THE *Curious* COOKBOOK

THE

Curious

COOKBOOK

Viper Soup, Badger Ham, Stewed Sparrows
& 100 More Historic Recipes

PETER ROSS

with a Foreword by Heston Blumenthal

THE BRITISH LIBRARY
and
MARK BATTY PUBLISHER

For Kier, Saskia and Sam

First published in 2012 by
The British Library
96 Euston Road
London NW1 2DB

and

Mark Batty Publisher LLC
68 Jay Street, Suite 201
Brooklyn, New York 11201
www.markbattypublisher.com

Cataloguing in Publication Data
A catalogue record for this publication is available from The British Library
Library of Congress Control Number: 2012932416

978 0 7123 5863 7 (British Library)
978 1 9356 1352 7 (Mark Batty Publisher)

Designed and typeset in Monotype Bulmer by illuminati, Grosmont
Printed in Hong Kong by Great Wall Printing Co. Ltd

Contents

Foreword

HESTON BLUMENTHAL

'TELL ME WHAT YOU EAT AND I WILL TELL YOU WHAT
YOU ARE' said the famous French gastronome Jean Anthelme
Brillat-Savarin (1755–1826). On the evidence of the pages in
this book, we humans are, among other things, experimental
('A cockatrice'), resourceful ('Candied sea-holly'), whimsi-
cal ('A dishfull of snow'), ingenious ('A cucumber stuffed
with barley to attract flies'), crude ('Whore's farts'), exotic
('Peacock roasted and served in its skin'), playful ('An artificial
jug or pitcher made of pork, cheese and bread') and seriously
omnivorous: there are recipes here for barbecued otter, viper
soup, porpoise with wheat porridge, chopped brain fritters,
pottage of tortoise and stewed sparrows on toast!

I find exploring the recipes of the past fascinating, but
it's a relatively new-found interest. I have to admit, with
some embarrassment, that up until about a decade ago I
had given little thought to British culinary history. The
way I got into it is a happy accident. I'm an impulsive and
compulsive acquirer of cookbooks and somehow I ended
up with a copy of a fifteenth-century manuscript collection
called *The Vivendier*, which included recipes for a fish with

flames coming out of its mouth, and a chicken that appears cooked but wakes up as it is about to be carved and makes off down the table 'upsetting jugs, goblets and whatnot'.

Naively perhaps, I had had no idea that recipes from the past could be so ambitious, so anarchic, so theatrical. I had to know more. So I attended the Oxford Symposium of Food and Cookery, an annual conference on food history that is edifying and esoteric in equal measure. That year, the subjects ranged from a presentation on Ming dynasty babyfood to theories of what might be eaten in a dystopia. My head reeling, I left the lecture hall to get some air and ended up talking to two men who not only knew *The Vivendier* but knew about lots of other bizarre dishes from the past, such as chicken cooked in the shape of a bottle.

I guess in truth it's not such a coincidence that, at a culinary conference in Oxford, I should end up taking a breather alongside two food historians from Hampton Court. Through them I met other historians and began reading works like *The Forme of Cury* and *The Art of Cookery Made Plain and Easy* (both of which feature in these pages), and of course *The Accomplish't Cook* by the incomparable Robert May, who is here memorably represented by recipes for pies containing live frogs and birds, a pastry stag that bleeds, exploding ships and castles, and a stew of palates, lips and noses of beef. Such books offered many unexpected insights into how food and cookery has evolved over time. *The Forme of Cury* (*c.* 1390), for example, has recipes for rice with saffron that anticipate Milanese risotto. In *The Art of Cookery* (1747), Hannah Glasse refers to 'Hamburg sausages', showing that the evolution of the hamburger was already under way in the eighteenth century. I've consulted them often while developing my own interpretations of recipes of the past, such as meat fruit, salamagundy, beef royal, quaking pudding and tipsy cake.

For a chef, of course, investigating old recipes and adapting them to a modern audience is a thrilling business. It establishes a connection to the past and offers the opportunity to carry on a grand tradition. And it's fascinating to have a window onto the way chefs of the past thought about food and worked with it. The levels of imagination and creativity of display – often with only the most rudimentary technology – are truly inspiring.

But I'd say the pleasure of books like *The Curious Cookbook* goes deeper than that. Because eating is such an intrinsic part of everyday life, the recipes of a particular period can reveal a lot about the social character of that time (albeit often at a high level: much of the culinary documentation from earlier centuries comes from the tables and household accounts of the rich and aristocratic rather than ordinary people). As you read on you'll notice, for example, how adventurous was our spicing of dishes in the medieval period – probably to introduce variety and interest to the limited number of ingredients on offer, particularly in the winter months – how much more in touch we were with the land and what it had to offer, and how much less squeamish we were about what graced the table. (The recipe for swan pie shows that not only was it once acceptable to eat the bird, it was also OK to wear the discarded skin as a fashion accessory!) Throughout, you gain a real sense of how cuisine isn't fixed but perpetually evolves, responding to trends, necessity, resources and access to new and exciting ingredients.

So, whether you're a keen cook who wants to try your hand at old, unusual or spectacular dishes, a connoisseur of the outlandish and bizarre recipes of the past, or simply someone who takes an interest in the intertwined culinary and social history of Britain, there's plenty to delight you on every page of this wonderful book.

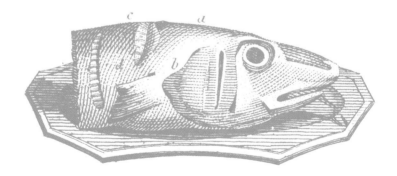

Introduction

ALL OF US CONSUME FOOD. But what we eat, or have eaten, differs across the world and through time. Today, one culture might consume dog with gusto and without sentimentality and yet feel physically sick at the thought of eating that rotting, mouldering lump of fermented cow's milk known as blue cheese. The same reaction can occur if we consider what people ate in the past, where fashion and availability of different foods are as important as geographical separation. This book provides examples of that very difference, and, by taking a look at the thousands of recipes written down from the fifteenth century to the Second World War, we quickly recognise that what we ate in the past now seems extraordinarily strange, intriguing, revolting, or just plain curious. Curiosity might have killed the cat, but it could not find a British recipe instructing us how to cook one. You will find, however, amongst others, recipes for peacocks, porpoises, cockscombs, larks, vipers, sparrows and starlings, squirrels' tails, minnows, tortoises, otters, plague water, cock-ale, swan pie, cowslip tart and badger gammon. You will learn how to roast a pound of butter, make pocket-soup, tell if a gull is fresh by pulling its leg, and how to stuff the swim-bladder of a cod.

Long before the advent of printing, what we ate in our medieval past was recorded in the handwritten accounts of the royal court and the households of the nobility. Usually these were simply lists of foodstuffs or menus from some significant meal or feast, and comprised little more than the names of dishes and the order in which they were served. But by the end of the fourteenth century, in society's highest strata, recipes emanating from the kitchens of professional male cooks were being recorded in some detail. Among the first of these was *The Forme of Cury* (c. 1390). Written at the behest of King Richard II, it naturally reflects the food eaten at court, rather than the very basic porridges, root vegetables and cheaper meats and fish that were eaten by the vast majority of the population. There are also a number of inter-related fifteenth-century documents, now part of the British Library's Harleian Manuscripts collection, which record similar high-class recipes. In these much abbreviated recipes it is often the strangeness of the ingredients that intrigue us now, along with the odd combinations of the sweet and the savoury. We might be horrified at the thought of eating a peacock or a porpoise, but these were once expensive, high-status foods. Many today would turn their noses up at those parts of the beast that delighted the medieval court, like the cockscomb or a cow's palate. Even the language used in these recipes can seem curious, charming and, occasionally, shocking. The medieval writer uses the pronoun *him*, instead of *it*, which renders some early recipes almost too personal – we are no longer divorced from the experience of eating a once-living animal when we read instructions like 'Take a Peacock, break his neck, and cut his throat' or 'take a porpoise and chop him as like salmon'. It is also in the medieval period that we encounter our ancestors' delight in the creation of highly decorative foods and dishes that trick and delight their guests rather than just feeding them. A number of such recipes are included here, like that for a pitcher or jug made of pork, cheese and bread, and for birds and animals cast in sugar, or, from a later period, the pies containing live birds and frogs. 'Four-and-twenty blackbirds baked in a pie' could quite easily have been a genuine recipe title.

The first recipe book printed in England was *This is the Boke of Cokery* (1500), but it was something of a rarity as

3

for much of the first three-quarters of the sixteenth century recipes were mostly included in more general works on domestic medicine, housewifery and 'good husbandry'. However, towards the end of that century a number of innovative London publishers collected together to publish books devoted almost wholly to cooking. These include *A Book of Cookrye* (1591) by 'A.W.', Thomas Dawson's *The Good Housewife's Jewel* (1596), the work edited by Sir Hugh Plat and published as *Delightes for Ladies* (*c.* 1602) and, just into the seventeenth century, Gervase Markham's wonderful *The English Hus-wife*. The last ran into thirteen editions between 1615 and 1683, reflecting the increasing popularity of cookbooks – a new cookery title appeared almost every other year between 1600 and 1700, which was more than twice as many as in the previous century.

Many of the foods eaten during the late Tudor period were similar to those of medieval times: roast and boiled meats and poultry, various pottages (soups or stews), cereal-based porridges, bread, and some cooked fruit and vegetables. On the whole very few people ate raw salads, fruit or vegetables as it was believed that they were not good for you. Various new foods had arrived throughout the sixteenth century, both from the New World and through increased trade with Africa and the Far East, which were being consumed by a broader section of the population – these included quinces, apricots, melons and, increasingly, citrus fruits. But by far the most dramatic change to diet during this period was the increased consumption of sugar, at least by the wealthier classes. It moved from being treated almost like a spice, used in tiny amounts, to become a major addition to desserts, jellies, fruit pastes and, in its purest form, decorated and moulded confections. Sugar's prominence was such that the wholly new profession of confectioner evolved at this time, first in the houses of the wealthy, then independently as shop owners and caterers.

The preparation of food and the ingredients used changed significantly during the seventeenth century. There were now greater numbers of wealthy people outside the aristocracy and nobility, those we might now describe as the middle classes, who had more leisure time and spare money to spend on food and entertaining. Many of these people lived in cities with access to more varied ingredients and less reliance on growing or raising their own food. Although the court continued to set the fashion for what was eaten, these fashions percolated down the social scale. Recipe books were no longer the preserve of the professional court cook, but were instead often intended for the gentlewoman running an increasingly urban household. It was just these sorts of women who, a century later, would come to write their own cookbooks and, for long periods, dominate the cookbook market.

New ingredients, some of which became staples of the British diet, were introduced in the seventeenth century. Chief among these were tea, coffee and chocolate. The 'fear' of raw salads ebbed away at this time too, until, in 1699, John Evelyn published *Acetaria: A Discourse of Sallets*, a book entirely devoted to the subject. Other types of food became more popular, including potatoes, biscuits, puddings and tarts. French cooking increasingly influenced English food, particularly after the Restoration of Charles II, who had been exiled in France, and the translation into English of La Varenne's books in the 1650s. This French influence led to the separation of sweet and savoury, which had up until this time often been mixed together and served at almost any stage in a meal. At the end of the century the focus of recipe books moved firmly away from country-house and court cooking and, with books like Hannah Wooley's *The Gentlewoman's Companion* (1673), probably the first printed English cookbook written by a woman, became almost exclusively aimed at the urban middle classes. William Rabisha's *The Whole Body of Cookery Dissected*, which has been described as one of the first 'modern' cookbooks, went through five editions in the twenty years after its publication in 1661 and remained influential right up to the middle of the eighteenth century. But some fashions took longer to change. Meals were still served in just a few, large courses, sometimes consisting

of many individual dishes all brought to the table at the same time, rather than one after the other as we would today. A first course might consist of a mixture of items, often including soups and roasted meats. These would all be removed and replaced with a second course, still consisting of mostly savoury dishes, including poultry, pies and vegetables, but there would also be some sweet tarts or fruit pies. A final course might consist of dried fruits and nuts, fresh fruit, cheese, and confectionery made with sugar.

In the early part of the eighteenth century, cookbook writers were mostly men, usually professional cooks who had worked in noble households and whose recipes reflected the prestige of their noble patrons. Among the most influential books of this period was the translation, from the French, of Massialot's *The Court and Country Cook* (1702), which introduced complex recipes containing several meats cooked together, served with strong sauces and often accompanied by many additions and garnishes – see for example Massialot's recipe for 'Sea-duck with chocolate in a ragoo'. Several publications, like Eliza Smith's *The Compleat Housewife* (1727), attempted to ape or simplify this style. Similarly, Charles Carter's *The Compleat City and Country Cook* (1732), whilst providing diagrams of table settings for elite city dinners, also includes cheaper and easier versions of these fashionable recipes. In contrast, one man who approached food from a different point of view, almost outside fashion, was the Oxford professor of Botany, Richard Bradley, whose somewhat eccentric publication *The Country Housewife* (1727) collected recipes from any source that interested him, including those printed here for 'viper soup' and 'A gammon of a badger roasted'.

By the middle of the eighteenth century women cookbook writers were the dominant force and Hannah Glasse's *The Art of Cookery Made Plain and Easy* (1747) was the great best-seller of the age. It is now recognised that she 'borrowed' many of her recipes from her contemporaries and, although she claimed to be hostile to the influence of French cuisine, plagiarised and adapted the style to suit English tastes and the pockets of her audience; her intention was that the book should be used by the mistress of the house to instruct her ignorant cook. Glasse offered shortcuts to achieve rich sauces and suggested ways to create dishes with decorative impact using simpler ingredients – see her recipes 'How to make an egg as big as twenty' and 'Fairy butter'. This continuing interest in decorative food is also reflected in Elizabeth Raffald's many recipes for dramatic edible centrepieces, like her hens and chickens set in jelly or her platter of gilded, floating, flummery fish.

The end of the eighteenth century and beginning of the nineteenth saw the publication of a number of books by London's professional male cooks at famous inns, like the London Tavern. The iconic dish served at such institutions was turtle soup, which was also consumed in vast quantities in livery halls and at Lord Mayor's banquets throughout the period. Some of the taverns had cellars full of live turtles waiting to be 'processed' into gallons of soup, or, later in the century, put into tins. But again female authors wrote the best-sellers of the age, first with Eliza Acton's *Modern Cookery for Private Families* (1845) and then the phenomenon

9

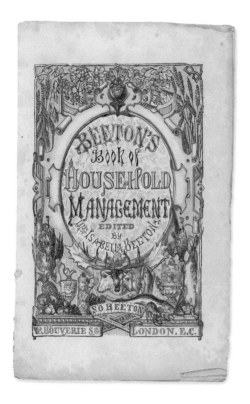

of Mrs Isabella Beeton's *Book of Household Management* (1861). Both women sought to provide wholesome meals, often costed down to the last penny, and, although the food could be seen as traditionally British, they were not afraid to incorporate new ingredients and ideas that were flowing into the country from the expanding empire.

In the twentieth century, some food writers came to regard Beeton's emphasis on economy and shortcuts as the beginning of a gradual decline in British cooking that would reach its nadir in the early 1950s. But these critics wilfully ignored the fact that Beeton's book is far more comprehensive than a frugal housewife's manual, including, as it does, complex recipes for veal, turbot, bird's-nest soup, jellies and ice creams, as well as recipes influenced by European and colonial cooking. In the twenty-first century, with the revival of British food, the increased use of offal, at least in restaurant food, and the reinvigoration of the English pudding, Beeton has gained her rightful place as an influential 'food writer' regardless of the fact that she may have borrowed her recipes from others, like almost every other food writer.

It is harder to look back on the twentieth century and find foods and recipes that we would now consider curious. Familiar with so many foods from around the world, we have become blasé about trying new things. But one significant period offers some intriguing recipes and takes us back to a time when people relied on basic ingredients often found by foraging – this was the 'Home Front' of the Second World War. At this time of food shortages and rationing, the government took control of the nation's nutrition and encouraged the population with numerous pamphlets and campaigns, embodied in the creation of Potato Pete and Doctor Carrot, to eat what could be most readily grown at home. They employed different tactics to make the food as interesting as possible, including one of the earliest collections of 'celebrity' recipes, *A Kitchen Goes to War: Famous People Contribute 150 Recipes to a Ration-time Cookery Book* (1940).

Despite the government's efforts to convince us otherwise, there really are a limited number of things you can do with potatoes, carrots, oats and the few luxuries available on the ration. Some writers recommended turning to 'wild foods' to supplement the dull, but famously healthy, wartime diet. For the first time possibly since the medieval period, it was suggested that the general public might like to partake of hedgehogs, rooks and songbirds. It is difficult to know now how many people followed the advice – indeed it is difficult to know how many people tried any of the recipes from this selection of six hundred years of cooking – but wealth and opportunity or poverty and hunger, or even just plain curiosity, must have caused at least some of our ancestors to chomp their way through porpoise or lark or tortoise, or indeed a steaming bowl of squirrel-tail soup.

NOTE   The recipes gathered here are for the most part taken unchanged from their original sources. A modern translation of recipes from medieval manuscripts has also been provided. The punctuation and spelling of the originals are mostly retained, unless they seriously obscure the meaning. Where a phrase or word's meaning is obscure, a translation or other editorial clarification is given in square brackets. With many of the early recipes the capitalisation of all nouns, common up until the eighteenth century, has been corrected to the modern form, retaining only those for proper nouns. Dates of works given in the introduction are the original publication dates; dates given after individual recipes refer to the edition of the work from which they were taken, and as such may differ.

Recipes

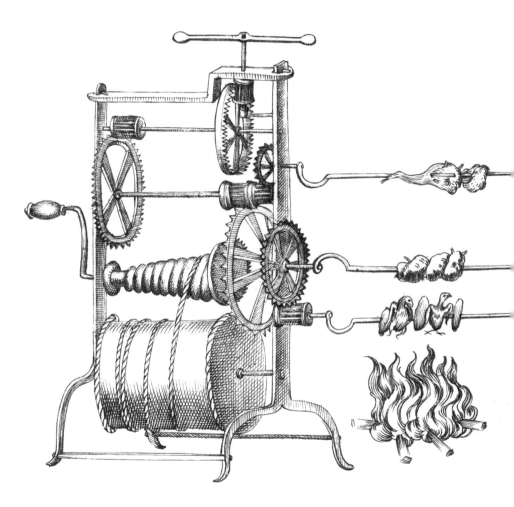

A medieval lasagne

Losyns. Take good broth and do in an erthen pot. Take flour of paynedemayn and make therof a past with water, and make therof thynne foyles as paper with a roller; drye it harde and seeth it in broth. Take chese ruayn grated and laye it in disshes with powdour douce, and lay theron loseyns isode as hoole as thou myt, and above powdour and chese and so twyse or thryse & serue it forth.

Lozenges. *Take good broth and put it in an earthenware pot. Take the best quality white flour and make a paste with water and make thin sheets with a rolling pin. Dry it until hard and boil it in broth. Take raw cheese grated and lay it in a dish with sugar and spice powder, and lay the lozenges as whole as you can, and above that more powder and more cheese, and so twice or thrice, and serve.*

The Forme of Cury, c. 1390

♣ A remarkably modern sounding dish that is clearly the ancestor of our modern lasagne. Much controversy surrounds the history of pasta. It had long been held that in the early fourteenth century Marco Polo brought pasta recipes back from his travels in the East. However, it would appear that noodles and other pasta-based foods were being consumed in Europe long before Polo's birth, possibly influenced by Arab and Roman cooking. The same source for this recipe also includes one for cheese-filled ravioli.

Preparing edible 'garbage' and 'compost'

GARBAGE. Take faire Garbage, chikenes hedes, ffete, lyvers, And gysers, and wassh hem clene; caste hem into a faire potte, And caste fressh broth of Beef, powder of Peper, Canell, Clowes, Maces, Parcely and Sauge myced small; then take brede, stepe hit in the same brothe, Drawe hit thorgh a streynour, cast thereto, And lete boyle ynowe; caste there-to pouder ginger, vergeous, salt, And a litull Safferon, And serve hit forthe.

GARBAGE. *Take fresh garbage, chickens' heads, feet, livers and gizzards, and wash them clean. Cast them into a good pot with fresh beef broth, powdered pepper, cinnamon, cloves, mace, parsley and sage minced small. Then take bread, soak it in the same broth, push it through a strainer and add it to the pot. Let it boil sufficiently and then add powdered ginger, verjuice* [sour grape juice], *salt and a little saffron. Serve.*

Harleian MS 4016, *c.* 1450

16

and wyn. and seson it vpp. and caste thereto a litul safferon to coloure
hit and salt / And serve hit forth ⁊

Bralune in penard

Take wyn ponder of Canell. bralbe hit thorgh a Streynoure. set hit
ouer the fire. lete hit boile. caste thereto. Macis. cloues. polbdey of
pep. take smale onyons hole. pboyle hem. caste they to. lete he boile
togider. then take Bralune. leche hit but not to thin. And if hit
be saused. let stepe hit in hote watter til hit be tendey. then cast hit
into þe sirype. take Saundres. vynegge. And caste thereto. And
lete boile al togidre. til hit be pnolbe. then take polbdey of gyng
caste thereto. lete hit not be to thik ne to thyn. butte as pottyge
shulde be. And serve hit forthe ⁊

Garbage ⁊

Take faire Garbage chikenes hedes. ffete. lyvers. And gysers
And wassh hem clene. caste hem into a faire potte. And caste fflessh
broth of Beef. polbdey of pep. Canell. Clolbes. Macis. prely
And Saunge myced smalt. then take brede stepe hit in þe same
brothe. Bralbe hit thorgh a streynoure cast they to And lete boyle
pnolbe. caste thereto poudey gyng. verge. salt. And a litill
Safferon And serve hit forthe ⁊

Pigge or chiken in Saune ⁊

Take a pigge Bralb him. stupte of his hede. kutte him in iiij.
guarteys. boyle him til he be pnolb. take him vpp. And lete cole
smyte him in peces. take an hondefull. or ij. of Saunge wassh
hit. grynde it in a mortey with hard yolkes of egges. then
bralbe hit vpp with goode vinegge. but make hit not to thynn
then seson hit with polbder of pep. gingey. and salt. then
colbche thi pigge in disshes. and caste þe sirup þ vpon and sue
hit forthe

Solbed Beeff. ⁊

Take faire ribbes of flressh beef And if thou wile roste hit

COMPOST. Take rote of persel, of pasternak, of rafens, scrape them and waische them clene. Take rapes and caboches, ypared and icorue. Take an erthen panne with clene water and set it on the fire; cast alle thise therinne. Whan they buth boiled cast therto peeres, and parboile them wel. Take alle thise thynges vp and lat it kele on a faire cloth. Do therto salt; whan it is colde, do hit in a vessel; take vyneger and powdour and safroun and do therto, and lat alle thise thynges lye therin al nyyt, other al day. Take wyne greke and hony, clarified togider; take lumbarde mustard and raisons coraunce, al hoole, and grynde powdour of canel, powdour douce and aneys hole, and fenell seed. Take alle thise thynges and cast togyder in a pot of erthe, and take therof whan thou wilt and serue forth.

COMPOST. *Take parsley roots, parsnips, radishes; scrape them and wash them clean. Take turnips and cabbages, pared and cored. Take an earthenware pan with fresh water and set it on the fire; put all these in. When they have boiled, add pears and parboil well. Take all these things out and let cool on a clean cloth. Add salt; when it is cold, place it in a vessel; add vinegar, powder and saffron, and allow to sit for a night and a day. Take Greek wine and honey, clarified together; take Lombard mustard and whole currants, and powdered*

18

cinnamon, sugar and spice powder and whole anise seed, and
fennel seed. Take all these things and place together in an
earthenware pot, and take out and serve as required.

The Forme of Cury, c. 1390

♣ Compost is a sauce or pickle of a type that the English have
long savoured. Very similar recipes can be traced back to
the writings of the Roman gourmet Apicius, who compiled a
cookbook in the first century AD, and forward into modern
times in the numerous recipes for chutney. It is also similar
to piccalilli, an English pickle of vegetables that in turn has
much in common with the Italian preserve of candied fruits
and mustard known as mostarda di frutta di Cremona.

The word 'garbage' has its origin in English in the kitchen
where, as here, it described those parts of a carcass that
might be thrown away, specifically the giblets – the gizzard,
liver, heart and neck of a fowl. It is hard to believe that any
edible parts of a chicken would have been thrown away
in most medieval households except those of the highest
status. Interestingly, the word 'garble' is seemingly related
as in medieval times this referred to the sieving of spices to
separate the best parts from those not required. Originally
meaning 'to take the best out of', it came to mean almost the
reverse – the mixing up or confusion of something.

Roasted milk

MYLKE ROSTYS. Take swete mylke, and do it in a panne; take eyroun with all the white, & swenge them, & caste there-to; colour it with safroun, and boyle it so that it wexe thikke; than draw it thorw a straynoure, and nym that leuyth, and press it: & and whan it is cold, larde it, & schere on schevres, & roste it on a gredelle, and serve forth.

MILK ROASTS. *Take sweet milk and put it in a pan. Take eggs with all the whites and mix them and add them, colour it with saffron, and boil it so that it thickens; then strain it through a strainer, and take what remains and press it. When it is cold, cut it and slice it in thin slices and roast it on a griddle and serve.*

Harleian MS. 279, *c.* 1430

♣ This recipe creates a type of delicate, twice-cooked custard, sliced when cold then roasted on a griddle. It demonstrates the sophistication of medieval court cookery, which required great skill to control the fires, chaffing dishes and charcoal burners that were utilised in the kitchen at this time. Without temperature-controlled ovens or hobs, the cook needed to attend to the fire constantly, adding fuel and moving the spits and cooking pots and pans towards or away from the heat source.

Hawthorn flower pudding

SPYNEYE. Take the flowtherys of hawthorun; boyle hem & presse hem, bray hem small, temper hem uppe with almaunde milke, and lye it with abyndoun and gratyd brede & flower of rys; take sugre y-now and put ther-to, or hony in defawte, & colowre it with the same that the flowrys ben, & serve forth.

SPINEY. *Take the flowers of hawthorn; boil them and press them, grind them small, mix them with almond milk and add wheat starch, grated bread and rice flour. Add enough sugar or honey, and colour it the same as the flowers, and serve.*

Harleian MS. 279, *c.* 1430

♣ Hawthorn flowers were so common in medieval recipes that dishes containing them were given their own name – 'spinee', presumably from the spines found on the shrub. The flowers, which have an almond scent, have in the past, along with the leaves, been eaten by country children, who called them 'bread and cheese'.

*A mythical beast created from
half a pig and half a cockerel*

COKYNTRYCE. Take a capoun, & skald hym, & draw
hem clene, & smyte hem a-to in the waste ouerthwart;
take a pigge, & skald hym, & draw hym in the same
maner, & smyte hem also in the waste; take a nedyl & a
threde, & sewe the fore partye of the capoun to the after
parti of the pygge; & the fore partye of the pigge, to the
hynder partye of the capoun, & than stuffe hem as thou
stuffyst a pigge; putte hem on a spete, & roste hym;
& whan e is y-now, dore hem with olkys of eyroun, &
pouder gyngere & safroun, thenne wyth the ius of percely
with-owte; & than serve it forth for a ryal mete.

COCKATRICE. *Take a capon* [a castrated cockerel], *and scald him; draw* [eviscerate] *him completely, and cut him in two around the waist. Take a pig, and scald him, and draw him in the same manner, and cut him also around the waist. Take needle and thread, and sew the fore part of the capon to the hind part of the pig, and the fore part of the pig to the hind part of the capon, and then stuff them as you stuff a pig. Put them on a spit and roast them, and when they are done enough, gild them with yolks of eggs, and powdered ginger and saffron, then pour over the juice of parsley; and then serve it for a royal feast.*

Harleian MS. 279, *c.*1430

♣ The mythical cockatrice has the head and legs of a cockerel and the tail of a reptile, dragon or snake. In England it is often confused with a basilisk – a serpent hatched from a cock's egg, fabled to kill with a single glance. This Frankenstein-like recipe combines two halves of different animals, stitched together in a monstrous, edible, heraldic table decoration.

An artificial pitcher
made of pork, cheese and bread

APPRAYLERE. Take the fleysshe of the lene porke, &
sethe it wel: & whan it is sothe, hew it smal; nym than
safroun, gyngere, canel, salt, galyngale, old chese, myid
brede, & bray it smal on a morter; caste thin fleysshe in
to the spicery, & loke that it be wil y-ground, temper
it vppe with raw eyroun; than take a longe pecher, al
a-bowte ouer alle that it be ransched; than held out thin
grece, & fulle thi pechir of thin farsure, & take a pese of
fayre canneuas, & doble it as moche as thou may ceuyr
the mouthe with-al, & bynd it fast a-bowte the berde, &
caste hym to sethe with thin grete fleysshe, in lede other
in cauderoun, for it be wyl sothin; take then vppe thin
pecher, & breke it, an saf thin farsure; & haue a fayre
broche, broche it thorw, & lay it to the fyre; & than haue
a gode bature of spicerye, safroun, galyngale, canel, therof y-now, & flowre, & grynd smal in a morter, & temper
it vp with raw eyroun, & do ther-to sugre of alisaunder
y-now; & euer as it dryit, baste it with bature, & sette
forth in servyce.

APPRAYLERE. *Take the flesh of lean pork, and boil it well;
and when it is boiled, cut it small; take saffron, ginger,
cinnamon, salt, galangal* [a kind of ginger], *old cheese, grated
bread, and grind it small in a mortar; then put the flesh into
the spice mixture, and see that it is well ground, mix it up
with raw egg. Then take a long pitcher, well rinsed out with
grease, and fill the pitcher with the stuffing, and take a piece of
clean canvas, and double it as much as you can over the mouth
of the pitcher, and bind it fast about the rim, and put it to boil
with your large joints, in a lead vessel or cauldron, so that it
is well boiled. Then take your pitcher, and break it, and save
your stuffing; and have a good spit, and spit it thoroughly, and
lay it to the fire; and then have a good batter of enough spices,
saffron, galangal, cinnamon and flour, and grind small in a
mortar, and temper it with raw egg, and apply to it enough
sugar of Alexandria; and as it dries, baste it with batter, and
then serve.*

Harleian MS. 279, c. 1430

♣ Medieval recipe books are full of instructions for disguising
foods that are often referred to as *solteties* – subtleties. They
were meant to trick or surprise the guests and came in
many forms, from sugar sculptures, roasted animals stitched
back into their skins as if they were still alive, to gilded
blancmanges and jellies moulded into fantastical shapes. Most
of the sugar in England was imported through Alexandria
and other Eastern Mediterranean ports, though much of it
was in fact grown further east.

Boiled minnows

MENESE OR LOCHE BOILED. Take menyse or loche, and pike hem faire; and make sauce of a gode quantite of ale and parcelly. And whan hit biginneth nye to boyle, skeme it clene, and cast the fish thereto; and lete seth. And if a man wol, cast a litul saffron thereto: and sauce is vergesauce. And then ye shall serve him forth hote.

MINNOWS OR LOACHES BOILED. *Take minnows or loaches, and pick them clean; and make sauce of a good quantity of ale and parsley. And when it comes up to the boil, skim it clean, and cast in the fish and let it boil. And, if you wish, add a little saffron, and the sauce is a sauce verte* [herb sauce]. *And then you shall serve it hot.*

Harleian MS. 4016, *c.* 1450

♣ Although the English rarely ate minnows, due mainly to their very small size, they would have been a welcome source of protein during times of food shortage. With harvests reliant on weather conditions and transport either non-existent or highly expensive, there were times when food became scarce, especially in the winter months. Many of the animals raised for meat were slaughtered towards the end of the year as there was little fodder available in winter months to keep them alive. The poorer sections of the population might rely on the fish they could catch in the rivers and around the coasts as a source of protein, whilst the wealthy would draw upon stocks of fish kept in ponds, or 'stews' as they were known. It is interesting to note that foods that were consumed in medieval times and then gradually fell out of favour were rediscovered in the twentieth century during the two world wars when other proteins may have been rationed.

27

Porpoise with wheat porridge

FIRMENTY WITH PORPEYS. Take faire almonds, and
wash them clene, and bray them with a mortar, and drawe
them with water thorgh a streynour into mylke, and
caste hit in a vessel. And then take wete, and bray it in a
mortar, that all the hole holl be awey, an boyle it in faire
water til hit be wel ybroke and boyled ynowe. And then
take hit from the fire, and caste thereto the mylke and
let boyle. And whan it is yboyled ynowe, and thik, caste
there-to sugar, saffron, and salt: Tehn then take a porpeys,
an chyne him as a samon, and seth him in faire water.
And whan hit is ynowe, baude hit, and leche hit in faire
peces, and serve hit forth with firmanty, and cast ther-on
hote water in the dish.

FRUMENTY WITH PORPOISE. *Take good almonds, and wash them clean, and grind them in a mortar and draw them with water through a strainer into milk, and place it in a vessel. And then take wheat, and grind it in a mortar, so that all the hull is removed, and boil it in fresh water until it is well broken up and has boiled enough. Then take it from the fire and add the milk and let it boil. And when it is boiled enough and thick, add sugar, saffron and salt; then take a porpoise, and joint him as you would a salmon, and boil him in fresh water. And when it is done, cut it, and slice it into fair pieces, and serve with the frumenty, and pour hot water into the dish.*

Harleian MS. 4016, *c.* 1450

♣ Porpoise, a generic term for several members of the porpoise and dolphin family, was in medieval times a very high-status meat, only available for the tables of the court, the aristocracy and the highest officers of the church. Although a mammal, it was regarded as a fish for the purposes of cooking and could therefore be consumed on days of fasting. Fish days, now considered as falling only on Fridays, were then far more numerous and could, if one were strictly pious, include both Wednesdays and Saturdays as well as numerous other fast days scattered throughout the year. Frumenty, a boiled wheat porridge, was traditionally served with porpoise and continued to be a popular accompaniment to many roasted meats well into the eighteenth century. For anyone wishing to reconstruct this recipe, the food historian Peter Brears suggests substituting tuna for the porpoise.

29

How to roast a peacock and
serve him in his skin

PECOK ROSTED. Take a Pecok, breke his necke, and
kutte his throte, And fle him, the skyn and the ffethurs
togidre, and the hede still to the skyn of the nekke, And
kepe the skyn and the ffethurs hole togiders; drawe him
as an hen, And kepe the bone to the necke hole, and roste
him, And set the bone of the necke aboue the broche,
as he was wonte to sitte a-lyve; And abowe the legges to
the body, as he was wonte to sitte a-lyve; And whan he is
rosted ynowe, take him of, And lete him kele; And then
wynde the skyn with the fethurs and the taile abought the
body, And serue him forthe as he were a-live; or elles pull
him dry, And roste him, and serue him as thou doest a
henne.

PEACOCK ROASTED. *Take a peacock, break his neck, cut his throat, and flay the skin and the feathers together, with the head still on the skin of the neck, keeping whole the skin and the feathers together; draw* [eviscerate] *him like a chicken, keeping the neck bone whole. Roast him, setting the bone of the neck above the spit, as if he were sitting alive; and the body above the legs, as if he were sitting alive. When he is roasted enough, take him off, and let him cool; and then wind the skin with the feathers and the tail about the body, and serve him as if he were alive. Or else pluck him clean, and roast him, and serve as you do a chicken.*

Harleian MS. 4016, *c.* 1450

❧ Peacock was another of the high-status meats eaten only at the very grandest of meals. Not being a species native to the British Isles, peacocks must have been raised on estates for the dual purpose of providing attractive animals to enhance the castle grounds and meat for banquets in honour of favoured guests. Nearly all of the early recipes provide instructions for re-dressing the roasted bird in its feathered skin, with its tail spread and comb gilded as if still alive. Peacock has been described as having a taste something between a chicken and a pheasant, but is often considered dry and tough. The food historian Peter Brears has noted that medieval illustrations of peacocks prepared for the table show them with fairly short tails; hence the birds would have been under eighteen months old and thus very tender and succulent. Peacock finally fell out of favour with the English nobility towards the end of the sixteenth century.

31

Imitation entrails

Trayne Roste. Take dates and figges, and kutte hem
in a peny brede; and then take grete reysons and blanched
almondes, and prik hem thorgh with a nedel into a threde
of a mannys length, and one of one frute and a-nother of
another frute; and then bynde the threde with the frute
a-bought a rownde spete, endelonge the spete, in maner
of an hasselet; and then take a quarte of wyne or ale,
and fyne floure, and make batur thereof, and cast thereto
pouder ginger, sugur, and saffron, pouder of clowes,
salt; and make the batur not fully rennyng, and nother
stonding, but in the mene, that hit may cleue, and than
rost the treyne abought the fire in the spete; And then
cast the batur on the treyne as he turneth abought the fire,
so longe til the frute be hidde in the batur; as thou castest
the batur there-on, hold a vessell vndere-nethe, for spilling
of the batur And whan hit is y-rosted well, hit wol seme a
hasselet; And then take hit vppe fro the spit al hole, And
kut hit in faire peces of a Span length, And serue of hit a
pece or two in a dissh al hote.

Train Roast. *Take dates and figs, and slice them as thin as
a penny; and then take large raisins and blanched almonds,
and prick them through with a needle onto a thread as long as*

a man, first one fruit and then another fruit; and then bind the thread with the fruit about a round spit, along the spit in the manner of a haslet. And then take a quart of wine or ale, and fine flour, and make a batter, and add powdered ginger, sugar, saffron, powdered cloves and salt; and make the batter neither runny nor thick, but in between, so that it will cleave. And then roast the train on the fire, on the spit; and then drop the batter on the train as it turns on the fire, until the fruit is hidden by the batter. As you drop on the batter, hold a vessel underneath, to catch any spilt batter, and when it is roasted well it will look like a haslet. And then take it up from the spit whole, and cut it in good pieces of a span's length, and serve a piece or two in a dish all hot.

Harleian MS. 4016, c. 1450

♣ A 'train roast' is one of the many medieval recipes that could be described as a counterfeit roast, as the intention here is to imitate a stuffed large-gut recipe known as a haslet, which was usually roasted on a spit. In this recipe for the train roast, layers of batter are built up around a string of fruits and nuts, creating a lumpy sausage that resembles the original stuffed gut. This dish has been successfully re-created by food historian Ivan Day, who describes the final stages of the process: 'The kitchen is filled with a wonderful smell of saffron and roasting batter. When the trayne roste has turned to a golden brown, the spit is taken away from the fire. If the thread is securely tied at each end, it pulls out of the cake when it is removed from the spit.'

To make one capon into two
by blowing up the skin

To Mak Capon in Cassolont. Tak a capon and
skald hym and opyn the skyn behynd the hed and blow
the skyn with a pen and raise it all about then tak pork
and hennes flesh and good pouders and mak a farsor ther
of and sew the skyn and parboille it then roll: the capon
and lard it and mak a batter of almond mylk and amydon
and colour it with saffron at the fyer and enbane it and
serue it.

To Make Capon in Cassolont. *Take a capon and scald
him and open the skin behind the head and blow the skin up
with a quill and raise it all over. Then take pork and chicken
flesh and good spices and make a stuffing, and sew the skin up
and parboil it. Then roll the capon and lard it with fat and
make a batter of almond milk and wheat starch and colour it
with saffron at the fire and baste it and serve it.*

A Noble Boke off Cookry, 1468

Eggs in moonshine

To Make Egges in Moneshyne. Take a dyche of rosewater and a dyshe full of suger, and set them upon a chaffyngdysh [*chafing dish*], and let them boyle, than take the yolkes of viii or ix egges newe layde and putte them therto everyone from other, and so lette them harden a lyttle, and so after this maner serve them forthe and cast a lyttle synamon [*cinnamon*] and sugar upon them.

Proper New Booke of Cokerye, 1545

✣ Another delicately performed recipe requiring precisely controlled cooking. It might be imagined that all medieval cooking was done on a spit or over an open fire, but many of the sauces, along with some boiled and fried foods, were prepared in pans heated over an earthenware pot containing burning charcoal known as a chafing dish. Here the cook could make a sauce, fry an omelette or create eggs in moonshine, which all required delicate heating. Today we might still encounter a chafing dish in one of those rather old-fashioned French restaurants that insists on preparing crêpes Suzette at the table – although the dish would usually be heated by gas or electricity rather than charcoal.

A dishful of snow

To Make a Dyschefull of Snowe. Take a pottell
[*four pints*] of swete thycke creame and the whytes of
eyghte egges, and beate them altogether wyth a spone, then
putte them in youre creame and a saucerfull of Rosewater,
and a dyshe full of Suger wyth all, then take a stycke and
make it cleane, and than cutte it in the ende foure square,
and therwith beate all the aforesayde thynges together, and
ever as it ryseth take it of[f] and put it into a Collaunder,
this done take one apple and set it in the myddes of it, and
a thicke bushe of Rosemary, and set it in the myddes of the
platter, then cast your Snowe uppon the Rosemarye and fyll
your platter therwith. And yf you have wafers caste some in
wyth all and thus serve them forthe.

Proper New Booke of Cokerye, 1545

♣ This delightful recipe takes careful reading to discover its
true nature. It begins with a meringue mixture to which is
added cream, rosewater and sugar until, with careful beating
and draining, it turns into a light, sweet mousse. A branch
of rosemary, supported in an apple, is placed at the centre of
the platter and then both the herb and platter are covered in
the white mousse in imitation of a lone, snow-covered tree
standing in a snowy landscape.

37

To cook shoes

To MAKE SHOES. Take a rumpe of beife and let it boyle an hower or two and put therto a gret quantitie of cole wurtes [*cabbages*] and let theim boile togither thre[e] howers then put to them a couple of stockdoves or teales [*a type of duck*], fesand, partrige or suche other wylde foules and let them boyle all togither then ceason them with salte and serue them forth.

Proper New Booke of Cokerye, 1545

♣ It is difficult to know where the shoes come into this dish as nothing in it seems to resemble any footwear, and nor does the end result. Given the inconsistencies of spelling in the sixteenth century we can only speculate on its original meaning.

A rabbit with a pudding in his belly

To Boyle a Cony with a Pudding in his Belly.
Take your cony [*rabbit*] and fley [*skin*] him, & leave on
the eares and wash it faire, and take grated bread, sweete
suet minced fine, corance [*currants*] and some fine hearbs,
peneriall [*pennyroyal*]; winter savery; percely [*parsley*],
spinage or beets, sweet margeram, and chop your hearbs
fine, and season it with cloves, mace and sugar, a little
creame and salt and yolks of eg[g]s, and dates minst fine.
Then mingle all your stuf togither, and put it in your
rabets belly and sowe it up with a thred, for the broth take
mutton broth when it is boyled a little, and put it in a pot
wheras your rabet may lye long waies in it, and let your
broth boile or ever you put it in, then put in gooceberies
or els grapes, corance and sweet butter, vergious [*sour
grape juice*], salt, grated bread and sugar a little, and
when it is boyled, lay it in a dish with sops [*slices of bread
or toast*]. And so serve it in.

A Book of Cookrye, 1591

39

A carp with fruit pudding in his belly

To Boil a Carp in Green Broth with a Pudding in his Belly. Take the spawn [*roe*] of a carp, and boil and crumble it as fine as you can. Then take grated bread, small raisins, dates minced, cinnamon, sugar, cloves, mace, pepper and a little salt, mingled together. Take a good handful of sage and boil it tender, and strain it with three or four yolks of eggs, and one white. Put to the spawn with a little cream and rose water. Then take the carp and put the pudding in the belly and seethe him in water and salt. When he is almost boiled take some of the spawn and of the best of the broth, and put it into a little pot with a little white wine, a good piece of butter, three or four onions, whole mace, whole pepper, small raisins, and three or four dates. When it is a good deal sodden, put in a good deal of seeded spinach, and strain it with three or four yolks of eggs, and the onions that you put in your broth. If it is too sharp put in a little sugar. And so lay your carp upon sops [*slices of bread or toast*] and pour your broth upon it.

Thomas Dawson, *The Good Housewife's Jewel*, 1596

♣ Many recipes from the sixteenth and seventeenth centuries involve stuffing a fish or an animal with a 'pudding in its belly'. The pudding is what we would today describe as either a stuffing or a forcemeat. A stuffing can serve a number of purposes; one made with fat might baste the meat from the inside and counteract any dryness, another might actually do the opposite and soak up excess fat, whilst a dull meat could be enlivened by a flavoursome filling. With meat and fish at a premium in many households, a stuffing would increase the bulk of dish and therefore serve more people from a single fish or rabbit. Both of these complex recipes belie the myth, often encountered in Hollywood movies, that Tudor food consisted only of joints of meat or chickens that the hungry kings and courtiers ripped apart with their hands and teeth, throwing the leftovers over their shoulder to the serfs and the dogs grovelling on the floor.

Stewed sparrows on toast

To STUE SPARROWES. Take good ale a pottel [*four
pints*], or after the quantities more or lesse by your
discretion, and set it over the fier to boyle, and put in your
sparrowes and scum the broth, then put therin onions,
percely [*parsley*], time, rosemary chopped small, pepper
and saffron, with cloves and mace, a fewe. And make
sippets [*bread, fried or toasted*] as you doo for fish, and laye
the sparrowes upon with the said broth, and in the seething
[*boiling or cooking*] put in a peece of sweet butter, and
vergious [*sour grape juice*], if need be.

A Book of Cookrye, 1591

♣ In the past, sparrows must have been eaten far more
often than might be expected in England, as evidenced by
the archaeological survival of sparrow-bottles, or birdpots,
particularly in London. The birdpot was a bottle-shaped
earthenware pot that could be hung on the outside of a house,
rather like a modern bird-box, in which sparrows could nest.
The birds entered and left the horizontal bottle by way of
the neck, but there was also an access hole at the rear, large
enough for the house owner to reach in and remove either the
eggs or, more likely, the nestlings. Archaeologists have noted
that birdpots have often been found in areas of high-class
housing, possibly indicating that the sparrow was a gourmet
morsel for the wealthy rather than a survival food for the poor.

42

A cockerel distilled with gold
for treating consumption

To STILL A COCK FOR A WEAKE BODY THAT IS
CONSUMED. Take a red cock that is not too olde, and
beate him to death, and when he is dead, fley [*skin*] him
and quarter him in small peeces, and bruse the bones
everye one of them. Then take roots of fenell, persely
[*parsley*], and succory [*chicory*], violet leaves, and a good
quantitye of borage, put the cock in an earthen pipkin
[*cooking pot*] and betweene everye quarter some rootes,
hearbes, corance [*currants*], whole mace, anis seeds,
being fine rubbed, and licorice being scraped and sliced,
and so fill your pipkin with al the quarters of the Cocke,
put in a quarter of a pinte of rosewater,
a pinte of white wine, two or three
dates. If you put in a peece of
golde, it will be the better, and
halfe a pound of prunes, and
lay a cover upon it, and
stop it with dough, and
set the pipkin in a pot
of seething [*boiling*]
water, and so let it

seethe twelve houres with a fire under the brasse pot that it standeth in, and the pot kept with licour twelve houres. When it hath sodden so many houres, then take out the pipkin, pul it open, and put the broth faire into a pot, give it unto the weak person morning and evening.

A Book of Cookrye, 1591

♣ This recipe distils the masculine strength of the cockerel, which in combination with herbs, spices and indestructible gold, will revive the weakened body of a consumptive with its medicinal 'essence'. Henry of Grosmont (*c.* 1310-61), author of *The Book of Holy Medicines,* associates the red cockerel with Christ and writes that 'the red cockerel is you, most sweet Jesus, who are, as I have said beforehand, physician and remedy'.

Fruit pudding in a hollowed-out turnip

How to Make a Pudding in a Turnep Root.
Take your turnep root, and wash it fair in warm water,
and scrape it faire and make it hollow as you doo a carret
roote, and make your stuffe [*stuffing*] of grated bread, and
apples chopt fine, then take corance [*currants*], and hard
egs, and season it with sugar, sinamon, and ginger, and
yolks of hard egs and so temper [*mix*] your stuffe, and put
it into the turnep, then take faire water, and set it on the
fire, and let it boyle or ever you put in your turneps, then
put in a good peece of sweet butter, and claret wine, and a
little vinagre, and rosemarye, and whole mace, sugar, and
corance, and dates quartered, and when they are boyled
inough, then will they be tender, then serve it in.

A Book of Cookrye, 1591

♣ This is a most unusual use of a turnip and is really more
like a recipe for stuffed apple, once a popular dessert but now
little encountered. The recipe instruction to 'make it hollow
as you do a carrot root' is intriguing. *A Book of Cookrye* does
contain a recipe for a stuffed carrot, this time adding goose
liver to the stuffing, but did our Tudor ancestors regularly
hollow out carrots for stuffing or simply remove the woody
centre when preparing carrots for any dish? Carrots at this

45

time were not necessarily large vegetables, as it was only
later that plant selection and breeding produced many of the
larger vegetables we know today. Nor were they necessarily
the orange colour we mostly encounter, but could be yellow,
white, red or even purple.

Portuguese puffs

To Make Farts of Portingale. Take a quart of life hony, and set it upon the fire and when it seetheth [*boils*] scum it clean, and then put in a certaine of [*sufficient*] fine biskets well serced [*sieved*], and some pouder of cloves, some ginger, and powder of sinamon [*cinnamon*], annis seeds and some sugar, and let all these be well stirred upon the fire, til it be as thicke as you thinke needfull, and for the paste for them take flower as finelye dressed as may be, and a good peece of sweet butter, and woorke all these same well togither, and not knead it.

A Book of Cookrye, 1591

❧ This recipe appears to have missed some final instructions, as later versions clearly show that a sweet choux-like pastry is intended, so that small puffs, resembling doughnuts, can be deep-fried. As these were light, hollow and full of air they were known in France as *pets* (French for farts) and later in England as 'whore's farts' (see p. 62) or, in the anti-Catholic eighteenth century, 'nun's farts'. By the time of the more prudish Victorians, these had become 'nun's sighs'. Portingale here means Portugal, and there might be a connection with the doughnut-like *churros* of Spain.

Candied sea holly

How to preserve Eringo roots, Aenula
Campana, and so of others in the same manner.
Seethe [*boil*] them till they be tender: then take away the
piths of them, and leave them in a colander till they have
dropped as much as they will: then having a thin sirup
ready, put them being cold into the sirup beeing also cold,
and let them stand so three daies, then boyle the sirup
(adding some fresh sirup to it; to supply that which the
rootes have drunke up) a little higher: and at three daies
end, boyle the sirup againe without any new addition,
unto the full height of a preserving sirup, and put it in
your rootes, and so keep them. Rootes preserved in this
manner, will eate very tender, because they never boyled
in the sirup.

Hugh Plat, *Delightes for Ladies*, *c*. 1602

♣ Candied sea holly, or 'eringo', as it was known, was once one of the major food products of the county of Essex, along with saffron, oysters and the long-forgotten and proverbially hard Essex cheese. Sea holly, *Eryngium maritimum*, still grows along the shores of Essex and many other counties, but it is no longer dug for its root, the part that was candied into 'kissing comfits'. This name shows that the candied roots had a reputation as an aphrodisiac, which was clearly known to Shakespeare; in *The Merry Wives of Windsor* Falstaff demands that the sky should 'hail kissing-comfits, and snow eringoes'.

Rabbits, woodcock and other animals cast in sugar

A MOST DELICATE AND STIFF SUGAR PASTE, WHEREOF TO CAST RABBETS, PIGEONS, OR ANY OTHER LITTLE BIRDE OR BEAST, EITHER FROM THE LIFE OR CARVED MOULDS. First dissolve issinglasse [*a gelatine made from fish bladders*] in faire water, or with some rose-water in the later end; then beat blanched almonds, as you would for marchpane stuff [*marzipan*], and draw the same with creame and rose water (milke will serve, but creame is more delicate): then put therein some powdered sugar; into which you may dissolve your issinglasse, being first made into gelly, in fair warm water (note, the more isinglasse you put therein, the stiffer your work will prove): then having your rabbets, woodcock, &c molded either in plaster from life, or else carved in wood (first anointing your woodden molds with oile of sweet almonds, and your plaister or stone moulds with barrows grease [*fat from a castrated male pig*]), pour your sugar-paste thereon. A quart of creame, a quarterne [*quarter*] of almonds, two ounces of isinglasse, and foure or six ounces of sugar, is a reasonable good proportion for this stuffe. You may dredge over your foule with crums of bread, cinamon and sugar boiled together, and so they will seem as if they were rosted and breaded. Leach [*set foods*] and gelly may be cast in this manner. This paste you may also drive with a fine rowling pin, as smooth and as thin as you please: it lasteth not long, and therefore it must bee eaten within a few daies after the making thereof. By this meanes, a banquet may bee presented in the forme of a supper, being a very rare and strange device.

Hugh Plat, *Delightes for Ladies*, *c.* 1602

♣ The casting or moulding of sugar figures and animals was popular in the medieval and early modern period among those who could afford to supply their household confectioners with enough of the very expensive imported sugar. As Hugh Plat describes, the moulds could be made of wood or plaster and often came in two or three pieces, with the final figure assembled by sticking the parts together. Plaster moulds were often created by taking castings from real fruits, vegetables and other objects, including even dead animals and birds. The final sugar sculptures would be painted and gilded and used to decorate the table or brought in for the final banquet course. Plat's recipe is closer to modern marzipan, which is still popular in Europe, moulded, modelled and coloured into numerous fruit, vegetable, animal and bird shapes.

Thirst-quenching fruit pastilles for ladies

To make a paste to keep you moist, if you list not to drink oft; which Ladies use to carry with them when they ride abroad. Take halfe a pound of Damaske prunes, and a quartern [*quarter*] of dates: stone them both, and beat them in a mortar with one warden [*cooking pear*] being rosted, or else a slice of old marmalade [*cooked fruit paste*]: and so print it in your moulds and dry it after you have drawne bread [from the oven]: put Ginger into it, and you may serve it at a banquet.

Hugh Plat, *Delightes for Ladies*, c. 1602

❧ Travellers in the early seventeenth century might not have cared to drink the possibly contaminated water they would encounter in rivers, streams and village wells, and would therefore have welcomed a pastille to alleviate their thirst until they reached an inn. Here they were more likely to drink beer or ale, as both the heating of the ingredients in the early stages of beer-making and the fermentation process created a drink that was safer to consume than water.

Camera propinqua alla Cu[...]

Conserua

POZZO

si passa il gielo

murello

lauorano de
Pasta

Candelier

passano sapori

Nutmegs candied for three weeks then smashed out of their pots

TO CANDIE NUTMEGS OR GINGER WITH AN HARD ROCK CANDY. Take one pound of fine sugar, and eight spoonfuls of rose-water, and the weight of six pence of gum Arabique, that is cleere: boyle them together to such an height, as that, dropping some thereof out of a spoon, the sirup doe rope and runne into the smallnesse of an haire: then put it into an earthen pipkin [*cooking pot*]; wherein place your nutmegs, ginger, or such like: then stop it close with a sawcer, and lute [*seal*] it well with clay, that not aire may enter: then keepe it in a hot place three weeks, and it will candy hard. You must breake your pot with a hammer, for otherwise you cannot get out your candy. You may also candy orenges or lemmons in like sort, if you please.

Hugh Plat, *Delightes for Ladies*, *c.* 1602

♣ In an age before frozen and tinned products, using sugar to candy or preserve foods was one of the major ways of keeping them available throughout the year. Ginger and nutmeg had long been imported into England in their dried form, along with ginger preserved in sugar. Hugh Plat may have got his recipe for candying nutmeg from a foreign source and may not have actually tried it out, as it would seem impossible that the rock-hard nutmeg could be candied soft enough to eat within three weeks. Had Plat actually obtained a garbled recipe and confused the ripened dried seed with the outside fruit? In the East Indies this part is indeed candied in sugar, after the mace and nutmeg have been removed. Surely Plat could not have obtained the fresh fruit in early-seventeenth-century England, given how long it would take to transport and the unlikelihood of its arriving in good condition?

Fruit preserved in pitch

FRUIT PRESERVED IN PITCH. Dwayberries that doe
somewhat resemble blacke cherries, called in Latine by the
name Solanum laethale, being dipped in molten pitch, being
almost cold, and before it congeale and harden againe, and
so hung up by their stalkes, will last a whole yeare.

Hugh Plat, *Delightes for Ladies*, *c.* 1602

♣ At the beginning of the seventeenth century, tar and the more
viscous pitch were among the chief exports of Sweden. Both
were made by heating or 'dry-distilling' pine wood, a process
that created both charcoal and turpentine as by-products.
Dwayberry is one of the names for the highly poisonous fruit of
the deadly nightshade, also known as belladonna and even as
'naughty man's berries'. Clearly this recipe was for a medicinal
purpose, but Hugh Plat's idea of preserving in pitch might
have come from his study of Roman writer Lucius Columella,
who had suggested that pitch could be used to preserve grapes.
Plat wrote extensively on ways of preserving food, including
wrapping lobsters in brine-soaked cloths and burying them
in sand, or covering pomegranates in wax and hanging them
from hooks. The latter is not dissimilar to the modern retail
practice of waxing lemons to lengthen their shelf life. Plat even
suggested preserving beef on long sea journeys by trailing it
behind the vessel in a barrel drilled with holes.

A cucumber stuffed with barley to attract flies

TO KEEP FLIES OFF YOUR PAINTINGS AND
HANGINGS. An Italian conceipte both for the rareness
and use thereof doth please me above all other: viz:
pricke a cowcumber full of barley corns with the small
spring ends outwards, make little holes in the cowcumber
first with a wooden or bone bodkin, and after put in the
grain, these being thicke placed will in time cover all the
cowcumber so as no man can discerne what strange plant
the same should be. Such cowcumbers to be hung up in
the middest of summer rooms to drawe all the flies unto
them, which otherwise would flie upon the pictures or
hangings.

Hugh Plat, *Delightes for Ladies*, *c.* 1602

❧ Hugh Plat, the collector of these recipes rather than the
original creator, does not quite make it clear that the wheat
stuck into the cucumber would quickly sprout and cover the
fruit in a coat of young shoots. This must have looked like
some exotic sea creature hanging from a chandelier at the
centre of a room. It would, no doubt, have grown increasingly
strange as the cucumber gradually dried and rotted, and the
barley shoots withered.

Butter roasted on a spit

To Roast a Pound of Butter Well. To roast a pound of butter curiously and wel, you shal take a pound of swete butter and beat it stiffe with sugar, and the yolkes of eggs; then clap it roundwise about a spit, and lay it before a soft fire, and presently dredge it with the dredging before appointed for the pig; then as it armeth or melteth, so apply it with dredging till the butter be overcomed and no more will melt to fall from it, then roast it brown, and so draw it, and serve it out, the dish being as neatly trimmed with sugar as may be.

Gervase Markham, *The English Hus-wife*, 1615

⚓ Markham's recipe for the dredging mixture, which he also uses when roasting a pig, combines fine breadcrumbs, currants, sugar and salt. This is constantly dredged over the butter and egg mixture on the spit, thus building up layers which finally create a sweet pudding that must have resembled a rich spotted dick with a crusty outside. This recipe has been successfully cooked by the food historian Ivan Day, who declared the dish delicious.

58

Dried instant vinegar for travellers

TO MAKE DRY VINEGAR. To make dry vinegar which you may carry in your pocket, you shall take the blades of green corn either Wheat or Rye, and beat it in a mortar with the strongest vinegar you can get, till it come to a paste, then roule it into little balls, and dry it in the Sun till it be very hard, then when you have occasion to use it cut a little piece thereof and dissolve it in Wine, and it will make a strong vinegar.

Gervase Markham, *The English Hus-wife*, 1615

♣ The key ingredient of vinegar is acetic acid. Markham's recipe concentrates and dehydrates this acid so that it can be used to make the wine taste sour like vinegar rather than actually turn it into vinegar. Vinegar was used as a sauce on hot vegetable dishes at this period, a fashion that really only survives today with the salt and vinegar we add to chips. It was also used, as it is today, in salad dressings.

Minnow, tansey, cowslip
and primrose omelette

MINNOW TANSEY. In the spring they make of them excellent minnow-tansies; for being well washed in salt, and their heads and tails cut off, and their guts taken out, and not washed after, they prove excellent for that use; that is, being fried with yolks of eggs, the flowers of cowslips, and of primroses, and a little tansy; thus used they make a dainty dish of meat.

Isaak Walton, *The Compleat Angler*, 1653

♣ A 'tansy' was an omelette-like pudding that took its name from the herb with which it was originally made – *Tanacetum vulgare*. The flavour of this yellow, button-flowered herb can be very strong, so only a small amount is called for, but so ubiquitous and popular were these herb recipes in earlier days that 'tansies' could be made without actually including any tansy at all. Cookery writer Elizabeth Ayrton, writing in 1974 of the Walton recipe above, declared that if you fish the minnows in a little stream in April and walk home through flowering fields in which you gather your cowslips and primroses, 'you will be eating the English spring'.

Sautéed tortoise with asparagus

POTTAGE OF TORTOISE. Take your tortoises, clean them
and cut them into pieces, fry them with a little butter,
parsley and spring onion having strained and seasoned
them well, simmer them in a dish with some stock on the
stove. Make sure you get rid of the turtle gall when you
cut them up, to insure your tortoises are clean and cook
well in the well-seasoned water. Simmer your bread also,
and then garnish it with your tortoises and their sauce,
with snapped asparagus around the dish, mushrooms,
truffles, slices of lemon and mushroom juice and serve.

La Varenne, *The French Cook*, 1653

♣ The books written by the French chef known as 'La Varenne'
were translated into English in the middle of the seventeenth
century and were at once highly influential. Indeed, one could
date the beginning of the English obsession with French food
from these translations. It became fashionable for the wealthy
to hire French chefs to cook in their households and to list
dishes in French on menus, both in private dining rooms
and, by the nineteenth century, in restaurants too. With
regard to this particular recipe, La Varenne may have had
access to tortoise in France, where it was native, but it would
seem unlikely that many English chefs would have had the
opportunity to cook this particular dish in its original form.

Whore's Farts

A VARIATION ON PORTUGUESE PUFFS. Make up your
fritter batter stiffer than ordinary by increasing the flour
and eggs, then set them out very small. When the fritters
are cooked, serve them hot with sugar and a savoury water.

La Varenne, *The French Cook*, 1653

♣ There is just a chance that these fritters may have got their
name not from their airy lightness, but from the fact that
many similar recipes require that the mixture be squeezed
into the hot oil or butter from a large syringe, the last
squirtful making the signature noise.

Barbecued otter

<small>SEA-OTTER ON THE GRILL.</small> Dress the sea-otter and roast it. When it is done, make whatever sauce you like for it, provided it tastes strong and, because the large pieces don't readily take on a flavouring, split it or slice it on top. Simmer it in its sauce until it has soaked up almost all of it. Then serve it, garnished with whatever you have on hand.

La Varenne, *The French Cook*, 1653

♣ Even though otters were once hunted for sport across the country, there appears to be no other recipe for otter in any English cookbook that could be traced. Interestingly, there is evidence of otter being eaten around this time in an early-seventeenth-century painting by the Flemish artist Frans Snyders. It depicts a fishmonger's slab covered in all types of fish, lobsters, crabs and shellfish and includes a very dead-looking otter alongside a more animated seal.

Pies containing live frogs and birds, a pastry stag that bleeds, exploding ships and castles

Make the likeness of a ship in paste-board [*cardboard*], with flags and streamers, the guns belonging to it of kickses [*odds and ends*], bind them about with packthread, and cover them with close paste proportionable to the fashion of a cannon with carriages, lay them in places convenient as you see them in ships of war, with such holes and trains of [*gun*]powder that they may all take fire; place your ship firm in the great charger; then make a salt round about it, and stick therein egg-shells full of sweet water.

Then in another charger have the proportion [*model*] of a stag made of course paste [*pastry*], with a broad arrow in the side of him, and his body filled up with claret-wine; in another charger at the end of the stag have the proportion of a castle with battlements, portcullices, gates and draw-bridges made of paste-board, the guns and kickses, and covered with course paste as the former; place it at a distance from the ship to fire at each other.

64

At each side of the charger wherein is the stag, place
a pye made of course paste, in one of which let there be
some live frogs, in each other some live birds; make these
pyes of course paste filled with bran, and yellowed over
with saffron or the yolks of eggs, guild them over in spots
... being baked, and make a hole in the bottom of your
pyes, take out the bran, put in your frogs, and birds, and

close up the holes with the same course paste... Being all placed in order upon the table, before you fire the trains of powder, order it so that some of the ladies may be perswaded to pluck the arrow out of the stag, then will the claret-wine follow, as blood that runneth out of a wound.

This being done with admiration to the beholders, after some short pause, fire the train of the castle, that the pieces all of one side may go off, then fire the trains, of one side of the ship as in a battel; next turn the chargers; and by degrees fire the trains of each other side as before. This done to sweeten the stink of powder, let the ladies take the egg-shells full of sweet waters and throw them at each other.

All dangers being seemingly over, by this time you may suppose they will desire to see what is in the pyes; where lifting first the lid off one pye, out skip some frogs, which make the ladies to skip and shreek; next after the other pye, whence come out the birds, who by a natural instinct flying in the light, will put out the candles; so that what with the flying birds and skipping frogs, the one above, the other beneath, will cause much delight and pleasure to the whole company.

Robert May, *The Accomplish't Cook*, 1660

Lips, noses, udders, ox-eyes
and sparrows on toast

To STEW PALLETS, LIPS, AND NOSES OF BEEF.
Take them being tender boild and blanched, put them
into a pipkin [*cooking pot*], and cut to the bigness of a
shilling, put to them some small cucumbers pickled, raw
calves udders, some artichocks, potatoes boil'd or musk-
mellon in square pieces, large mace, two or three whole
cloves, some small links or sausages, sweetbreads of veal,
some larks, or other small birds, as sparrows, or ox-eyes,
salt, butter, strong broth, marrow, white-wine, grapes,
barberries [*fruit of the shrub berberis*], or gooseberries,
yolks of hard eggs, and stew them all together, serve them
on toasts of fine French bread, and slic't lemon; sometimes
thicken the broth with yolks of strained eggs and verjuyce
[*verjuice, sour grape juice*].

Robert May, *The Accomplish't Cook*, 1660

♣ Robert May's book records food that was prepared in
the wealthier houses of seventeenth-century England,
and it is clear from this recipe that the nobility did not
disdain the cheaper cuts of meat at the dinner table. Few
today would knowingly eat palates, lips and noses, though
all of these parts will find their way into cheap sausages

and other products made from 'mechanically recovered meat'. May recognised that with careful preparation these often flavoursome parts of an animal could be turned into sophisticated dishes. He also incorporates potatoes, an unusual addition for such an early recipe, as the vegetable was not regularly eaten until well into the next century.

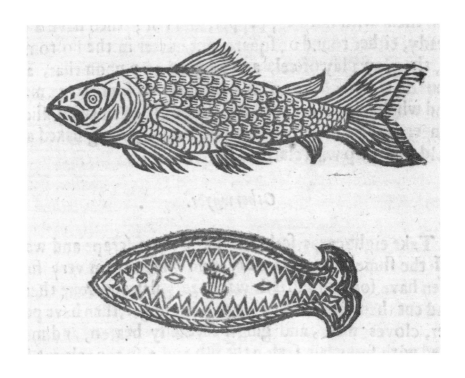

Fishy mince pies

TO MAKE MINCED PIES OF CARPS AND EELS. Take
a carp being cleansed, bone it, and also a good fat eel,
mince them together, and season them with pepper,
nutmeg, cinamon, ginger, and salt, put to them some
currants, caraway-seed, minced orange-peel, and the yolks
of six or seven hard eggs minced also, sliced dates, and
sugar; then lay some butter in the bottom of the pyes, and
fill them, close them up, bake them, and ice them.

Robert May, *The Accomplish't Cook*, 1660

♣ In the first half of the seventeenth century the English
continued to delight in combinations of sweet and savoury,
even mixing dried fruits, such as the dates and currants
included here, with fish. This recipe has echoes of the
Russian pie *kulebyaka*, or coulibiac, which combines fish
with boiled eggs and occasionally includes the addition
of dried fruits. Throughout the sixteenth and seventeenth
centuries all sort of pies, including meat and fish pies, were
finished with a sugar icing and the pie was returned to the
oven to set the icing and produce a shiny surface to the top.

69

A cure for the plague

To Make Plague Water. Take rue, agrimony, wormwood, celandine, sage, balm, mugwort, dragons, pimpernel, marigold, fetherfew, burnet, sorrel, and elecampane-roots scraped and sliced small, scabious, wood-betony, brown may-weed, mints, avence, tormentil, carduus benedictus, and rosemary as much as any thing else, and angelica if you will. You must have like weight of all them, except rosemary aforesaid, which you must have twice as much of as of any of the rest; then mingle them all together and shred them very small; then steep them in the best white-wine you can get three days and three nights, stirring them once or twice a day, putting no more wine than will cover the herbs well; then still it in a common still, and take not too much of the first water, and but a little of the second, according as you feel the strength, else it will be sour. There must be but half as much elecampane as of the rest.

The Closet of the Eminently Learned Sir
Kenelme Digby Kt. Opened, 1669

♣ Plague would still have been a major concern to those who had lived through the dreadful epidemic of 1665. But Kenelme Digby and his contemporaries could not have known that the Great Plague of that year was actually England's last major plague epidemic.

To bottle cock ale

TO MAKE COCK-ALE. Take eight gallons of ale, take a cock and boil him well; then take four pounds of raisins of the sun well stoned, two or three nutmegs, three or four flakes of mace, half a pound of dates; beat these all in a mortar, and put to them two quarts of the best sack [*white fortified wine*]: and when the ale hath done working, put these in, and stop it close six or seven days, and then bottle it, and a month after you may drink it.

The Closet of the Eminently Learned Sir Kenelme Digby Kt. Opened, 1669

♣ Samuel Pepys records in his diary that on 2 February 1663 he drank a cup of cock ale, but he provides no comment on what he thought of the drink. It is unclear what the cockerel brings to this beer, other than turning an ordinary ale into one for 'real men' – the sort of person who would rise to the challenge of eating the hottest curry or chilli con carne and pretend it was still rather too mild. Very similar recipes suggest putting the ground-up cockerel, bones and all, into a canvas sack before suspending it in the ale. However, one modern version has a warning attached: 'Brewers considering making their own cock ale should probably take extra precautions to avoid microbiological contamination of their beer.'

Slices of bacon imitated in marzipan

To Make Collops like Bacon of Marchpane.
Take some of your marchpane [*marzipan*] Paste, and work
it in red saunders [*sandalwood – a red dye*] till it be red;
then rowl a broad sheet of white paste, and a sheet of red
paste; three of the white and four of the red, and so one
upon the other in mingled sorts, every red between, then
cut it overthwart, till it look like collops [*slices*] of bacon,
then dry it.

A Queen's Delight, 1671

♣ This is one of the most popular recipes of the seventeenth
century, appearing in both printed and manuscript recipe
books. The fashion for disguising one food to look like
another dates back to medieval times, but became particularly
popular in the sixteenth century with the development of the
banquet course, which came at the end of the meal. Diners
would often retire to another room, or even to a specially
built banqueting house, where they would enjoy decorated
and moulded foods made from sugar, fruits and spices. In
this recipe, marzipan coloured both red and white is rolled
together and sliced across to look like rashers of streaky
bacon. The conceit survives today in seaside sweet rock shops
where you can still buy plates of bacon and eggs or sausages
made from coloured sugar.

A great swan pie
and a swan-skin stomacher

TO BAKE A SWAN. Pull all the gross feathers from the swan clean, and all the down; then case [*skin*] your swan, and bone it, leave all the flesh, lard it [with fat] extreme well, and season it very high with pepper, salt, cloves, and mace; so having your coffin [*pastry case*] prepared in the proportion of the swan, make of rye dough, put in your swan, and lay some sheets of lard and bay-leaves on top,

so put on butter and close it: put on the head and legs on the top, garnish and indore [*gild*] it, and bake it; when it is cold fill it up with clarified butter. Your skin being spread forth and dried, is good to make a stomacher for them that are apt to take cold in their breast.

William Rabisha, *The Whole Body of Cookery Dissected*, 1682

♣ Swan was eaten in England from early medieval times and was often thought of as the preserve of the very wealthy. Usually roasted, and often re-dressed in its skin (see roasted peacock on p. 30), this particular recipe is for a great pie filled with boneless swan meat that is sealed with butter poured through the vent hole of the pie. With the skin no longer needed in the recipe, Rabisha suggests it be used as a fashion accessory. Swan fell out of favour shortly after this time, replaced on special occasions or feast days by the recently introduced and easily domesticated turkey.

A sweet and spicy potato and fruit pie

To Make a Potato Pie. Boyle your Spanish potatoes (not overmuch) cut them forth in slices as thick as your thumb, season them with nutmeg, cinnamon, ginger, and sugar; your coffin [*pastry case*] being ready, put them in, over the bottom, add to them the marrow of about three marrow-bones, seasoned as aforesaid, a handful of stoned raisons of the sun, some quartered dates, orangado [*candied orange peel*], cittern [*candied citron peel*], with ringo-roots [*candied root of eringo or sea holly*] sliced, put butter over it, and bake them: let their lear [*a thickened sauce*] be a little vinegar, sack [*white fortified wine*] and sugar, beaten up with the yolk of an egg, and a little drawn butter; when your pie is [cooked] enough, pour it [*the sauce*] in, shake it together, scrape on sugar, garnish it, and serve it up.

William Rabisha, *The Whole Body of Cookery Dissected*, 1682

♣ Modern potato recipes are usually confined to savoury dishes. It is unclear if the Spanish potatoes referred to in this very early recipe are sweet or ordinary potatoes, both of which arrived in Europe, for the most part, via Spain. Seventeenth-century recipes still often combined sweet and savoury elements and even wholly savoury pies containing meat could be iced with sugar at the final stages.

76

A tart made with a gallon
of cowslip flowers

To MAKE A COWSLIP TART. You must take the
blossoms, of at least a gallon of cowslips, mince them
exceeding small, and beat them in a mortar, put to them
a handful or two of grated naples-bisket [*similar to sponge
fingers or macaroons*], about a pint and half of cream,
so put them into a skillet, and let them boyle a little on
the fire, take them off, and beat in eight eggs with a little
cream, if it doth not thicken, lay it on the fire gently until
it doth, take heed it curdles not, season it with sugar,
rosewater; and a little salt; you may bake it in a dish, or
little open tarts, but your best way is to let your cream be
cold before you stir in your eggs.

William Rabisha, *The Whole Body of Cookery Dissected*, 1682

♣ This delightful custard tart contains a staggering quantity
of cowslip flowers, which clearly must have been more
common in the hedgerows and fields of seventeenth-century
England than they are today. Flowers have long been
consumed both as an ingredient and as decoration. The
diarist John Evelyn, whose writing is contemporary with this
recipe, recommended the inclusion of primrose flowers in
salads, and Sir Hugh Plat included recipes for crystallising

77

these flowers whilst they were still growing on the plant. Florence White in *Flowers as Food* (1934) lists cowslip cream, syrup, tea, wine and mead, as well as cowslip cake, cowslip pickle, cowslip vinegar and an early-eighteenth-century recipe for honeycomb cakes of cowslips. In Essex, where cowslips were once known as 'paigles', the dried petals were mixed with flour and made into 'paigle puddings'.

A pickle of green ash keys

To PICKLE ASHEN KEYS. Take the youngest keys [*seed bract of the ash tree*] in May, when they are full-grown and tender, put them in a liquor made of half vinegar and water, and some salt; put no more upon them than what will cover them; set them upon hot embers, but let them not boyl; stir them often and they will be first yellow; keep them stirred until they be green, then take them out, and lay them abroad upon a board until they be cold, then put them up in fresh vinegar and salt, with a piece of alum. Cover the crock close, with a weight upon it.

The Queen's Closet Opened, 1696

♣ Ash keys, which were held in high esteem by physicians in classical times, are the only really edible portion of the tree, although a tea can be made from the leaves. The diarist and writer John Evelyn included a very similar recipe to the one given here in his book *Acetaria: A Discourse of Sallets* (salads) of 1699. The pickled keys can be used as a substitute for capers.

79

A sea-duck served with a sauce of chocolate, truffles and morels

A SEA-DUCK WITH CHOCOLATE IN A RAGOO. Having pick't, cleans'd and drawn your sea-duck, as before, let it be wash'd, broiled a little while upon the coals, and afterwards put in a pot; seasoning it with pepper, salt, bay-leaves and a faggot [*bundle*] of herbs. Then a little chocolate is to be made and added thereto; preparing at the same time a ragoo [*from the French ragout, or stew*] with capons-livers, morilles [*morel mushrooms*], mousserons [*the sweetbread mushroom*], common mushrooms, truffles, and a quarter of a hundred of chestnuts. When the sea-duck is ready dress'd in its proper dish, pour your ragoo upon it; garnish it with what you please, and let it be serv'd up to table.

François Massialot, *The Court and Country Cook*, 1702

♣ There are several species that would now be described as a 'sea-duck', including eiders, scoters, goldeneyes and mergansers. The use of chocolate as a seasoning in savoury dishes is more commonplace in South American cooking, but the French chef Massialot may have been influenced by Italian cooks when he created this dish, as they had been experimenting with the addition of small amounts of chocolate in meat dishes in the 1680s. Massialot's books, first published in France in the 1690s, were translated into English and published in London as *The Court and Country Cook* in 1702. This particular recipe seems not to have influenced English dining habits and chocolate remained a rare addition to savoury foods in England until the arrival of Mexican restaurants in the late twentieth century.

Badger ham anyone?

A GAMMON OF A BADGER ROASTED. The badger is
one of the cleanest creatures, in its food, of any in the
world, and one may suppose that the flesh of this creature
is not unwholesome. It eats like the finest pork, and is
much sweeter than pork. Then, just when a badger is
killed, cut off the gammons, and strip them; then lay
them in a brine of salt and water, that will bear an egg,
for a week or ten days then boil it for four or five hours,
and then roast it, strewing it with flour and rasped bread
[*breadcrumbs*] sifted. Then put it upon a spit... Serve
it hot with a garnish of bacon fry'd in cutlets, and some
lemon in slices.

Richard Bradley, *The Country Housewife
and Lady's Director*, 1736

❧ Richard Bradley, an Oxford professor of botany as well
as author of manuals for housewives, must have considered
this recipe, given to him by a 'Mr. R.T.' of Leicestershire, a
curiosity, as he inserted it into his book immediately after
a series of French recipes for cooking frogs and snails.
There are very few recipes for cooking badger, which has
been said to taste like a gamey beef and might be best
eaten curried. However, another interesting badger recipe

survives in a collection of rustic provincial French recipes called *Les cuisines oubliées*, which starts with the splendid instruction 'Eviscerate and skin your badger, and soak it in a fast-flowing river for at least 48 hours. This will help you to de-grease it more easily.'

Viper soup, or viper and snail broth – the choice is yours

VIPER SOUP. Take vipers, alive, and skin them, and cut off their heads; then cut them in pieces, about two inches in length, and boil them, with their hearts, in about a gallon of water to eight vipers, if they are pretty large. Put into the liquor a little pepper and salt, and a quart of white wine to a gallon of liquor; then put in some spice, to your mind, and chop the following herbs, and put into it: take some ghervill [*chervil*], some white beet-cards [*chard*] or leaves, some hearts of cabbage-lettuce, a shallot, some spinach leaves, and some succory [*chicory*]. Boil these, and let them be tender; then serve it up hot, with a French [*bread*] roll in the middle, and garnish with the raspings of bread [*breadcrumbs*] sifted, and slices of lemon.

Richard Bradley, *The Country Housewife and Lady's Director*, 1736

VIPER BROTH. Get two vipers and cut them in sixteen pieces, but use not the heads, skin them and season with mace salt and Jamaica pepper [*allspice*], put to two vipers, two quarts of good fish-broth, or clear veal-broth, or water, according as you will have it strong, stew this half away, and strain it, put in a faggot [*bundle*] of herbs and one shallot. A way to make snail broth is with snails washed and shelled and rubbed with water and salt, then stew them from two quarts of water to one, and then strain them off and season the same as the viper broth, and it is good for consumption.

Charles Carter, *The Compleat City and Country Cook*, 1736

♣ Although snakes were, and still are, eaten on all five continents, viper soup seems to have enjoyed only a short vogue in England. Richard Bradley acquired his recipe from the same Frenchman who supplied the recipes for snails in various sauces and fricassees. Viper broth, as opposed to viper soup, was a much more common medicinal recipe that is found in housewife and herbal manuals from the sixteenth to the nineteenth centuries. It was said to be an antacid as well as a strengthening and restorative tonic, which usually indicates that it was believed to restore a failing libido.

A jellied rock pool complete with fish, shells and seaweed

GURNETS, GUDGEONS AND OYSTERS IN ROCK JELLY.
Boil them in a good corbullion [*poaching liquid*], but not
to pieces; let them be all whole, and make a good jelly
of gurnets, eels, flounders, scate, and whiting; then put
a little at the bottom of a deep bason, and when cold lay
two or three small oyster-shells, and some of the sea-weed,
with two or three crayfish; then some jelly, then a row of
gudgeons, then perch, then jelly, till your bason is full:
let it stand till cold and stiff, and turn it all out whole;
garnish with lemons, raw parsly and fennel.

Charles Carter, *The Compleat City and Country Cook*, 1736

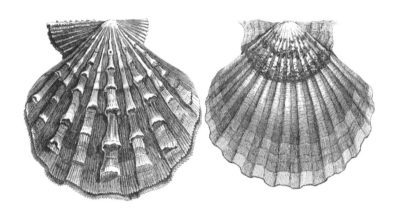

86

♣ Anyone who has recently eaten at Heston Blumenthal's Fat Duck at Bray restaurant may recognise an affinity between this edible rock-pool dish and his famous 'Sound of the Sea'. Both seek to create the atmosphere of a seaside pool, though Blumenthal adds a layer unavailable to Charles Carter by supplying an iPod for each diner with a recording of sea sound effects. That there should be a connection between these dishes ought not to be a surprise, as Blumenthal is a scholar of food history who has long searched cookbooks of the past for inspiration. His latest venture, Dinner, is a restaurant inspired by British gastronomy, where each dish listed on the menu is dated to show the period that has influenced its creation.

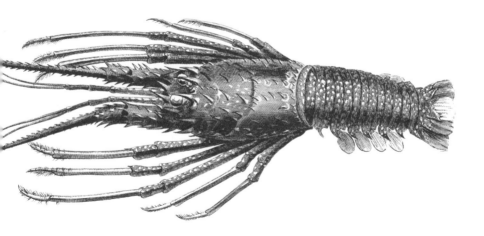

Larks, served in a nest of eggs
or shaped like a pear with
their feet as a stalk

LARKS IN SHELLS. Boil twelve hen or duck eggs soft; take out all the inside, making a handsome round at the top [of the shell]; then fill half the shells with passed [*sieved*] crumbs, and roast your larks; put one in every shell, and fill your plate with passed crumbs brown[ed]; so serve as eggs in shells.

LARKS PEAR FASHION. Truss your larks close, and cut off the legs and season them with pepper, salt, cloves and mace; then make a good force-meat [*stuffing*] with sweetbread, morelles [*morel mushrooms*], mushrooms, crums, egg, parsly, thyme, pepper and salt after which put in some suet and make it up stiff; then wrap up every lark in force-meat, and make it pointed like a pear and stick the leg a top; they must be washed with the yolk of an egg and crums of bread bake them gently, and serve them with-out sauce or they will serve for a garnish.

Charles Carter, *The Compleat City and Country Cook*, 1736

♣ The skylark is now a protected species, but in the past it was much favoured for its delicate flavour when roasted on a spit or made into pâté. In our more squeamish, and possibly more sentimental, age some would be horrified at the thought of eating lark, especially one moulded into a meaty pear with its spindly leg sticking out of the top. Even in the nineteenth century, one writer said that stripped of its wings, feet and gizzard the carcass of a lark resembled nothing more than a bundle of toothpicks.

Baked wheatears potted in butter

POTTED WHEAT-EARS. They are a Tunbridge bird;
pick them very clean, season them with pepper and salt,
put them in a pot, cover them with butter and bake them
one hour; take them and put them in a cullender to drain
the liquor away, then cover.

Charles Carter, *The Compleat City and Country Cook*, 1736

❧ In the past, small birds of many kinds must have ended
up in the cooking pots of the poorer sections of the rural
population to supplement their meagre protein intake, as is
still the case in some southern European countries, despite
EU regulations. The wheatear, a small migratory bird
now regarded as a member of the flycatcher family (and
presumably once common around Tunbridge in Kent), was
a favoured 'light snack' right up until the later nineteenth
century. The modern diner might regard the consumption of
songbirds as horrific and yet think nothing of chomping on
the similarly sized quail, served with foie gras atop a piece of
fried bread.

Calves feet served with a sweet currant and cream sauce

CALF'S FEET SWEET. You must boil them tender and take out the bones; then plump some currants, and put in half a pint of cream and the yolks of two eggs, a little melted butter and sugar, so serve away hot.

Charles Carter, *The Compleat City and Country Cook*, 1736

Little dishes of mushroom-stuffed cockscombs in gravy

TO FORCE COCKS-COMBS. Parboil your cocks-combs, then open them with a point of a knife at the great end: take the white of a fowl, as much bacon and beef marrow, cut these small, and beat them fine in a marble mortar; season them with salt, pepper, and grated nutmeg, and mix it with an egg; fill the cocks-combs, and stew them in a little strong gravy softly for half an hour, then slice in some fresh mushrooms and a few pickled ones; then beat up the yolk of an egg in a little gravy, stirring it. Season with salt. When they are enough, dish them up in little dishes or plates.

Hannah Glasse, *The Art of Cookery Made Plain and Easy*, 1747

♣ The cockscomb, which featured in many early recipes both as an ingredient and on its own, is here stuffed with a rich forcemeat and served as a side dish. Similarly, Charles Carter's calves' feet recipe dresses a simple and cheap food in a sweet cream sauce, turning it into a sophisticated dish. In the past most diners were less squeamish about eating almost any part of an animal. Organs and parts of the body that we would now throw away in favour of breast meat, fillet or leg were once highly savoured. The poorer the society the more highly they regarded the nutritional value of liver, blood and fat. In the few remaining hunter–gatherer societies, at the scene of a fresh kill, the most prized organs, like the liver, might be handed to the most honoured member of the group to eat raw. In times of food restrictions fat was savoured, offal was utilised, and the extremities, like heads and trotters, processed into much-savoured dishes. There has been a recent revival in the use of offal, famously championed by Fergus Henderson at his London restaurant St John and in his cookbook *Nose to Tail Eating*.

Kebabs of ox palate, pigeon, chicken-peepers, cockscombs and oysters

To Roast Ox Palates. Having boiled your palates
tender, blanch them, cut them into slices about two
inches long, lard [*insert strips of fat*] half with bacon,
then have ready two or three pigeons and two or three
chicken-peepers [*very young chickens*], draw [*eviscerate*]
them, truss them, and fill them with force-meat [*stuffing*];
let half of them be nicely larded, spit them on a bird-spit:
spit them thus: a bird, a palate, a sage-leaf, and a piece of
bacon; and so on, a bird, a palate, a sage-leaf, and a piece
of bacon. Take cocks-combs and lambs-stones [*testicles*],
parboiled and blanched, lard them with little bits of
bacon, large oysters parboiled, and each one larded with a
piece of bacon, put these on a skewer with a little piece of
bacon and a sage-leaf between them, tie them on to a spit
and roast them, then beat up the yolks of three eggs, some
nutmeg, a little salt and crumbs of bread; baste them with
these all the time they are a-roasting, and have ready two
sweetbreads each cut in two, some artichoke-bottoms cut
into four and fried, and then rub the dish with shalots:
lay the birds in the middle, piled upon one another, and
lay the other things all separate by themselves round

about in the dish. Have ready for sauce a pint of good gravy, a quarter of a pint of red wine, an anchovy, the oyster liquor, a piece of butter rolled in flour; boil all these together and pour into the dish, with a little juice of lemon. Garnish your dish with lemon.

Hannah Glasse, *The Art of Cookery Made Plain and Easy*, 1747

♣ Glasse's recipe for 'surf and turf' kebabs reminds us that the skilled cooking of food on a spit in front of a fire is a lost art in much of northern Europe and America. Until the later nineteenth century, most meat, some fish and occasionally other foods were cooked on a spit turned either by a clockwork jack, by hand, or even by a dog in a spit wheel. An experienced cook knew when the fire was at the right temperature, how far to set the spit from the heat source, and what bastings to use. Meats cooked in this way would often receive a final dredging of breadcrumbs, spices and eggs to build up a crust that was regarded by many as the finest part of the dish. Any cook who allowed the meat to burn or cinders to fall in the dripping tray was not worthy to 'rule the roast'. Again, Heston Blumenthal is contributing to the revival of this method, as his Dinner restaurant in London features many spit-roasted foods.

Instant meat-stock 'glue'
to carry in your pocket

To Make Pocket-Soup. Take a leg of veal, strip off
all the skin and fat, then take all the muscular or fleshy
parts clean from the bones. Boil this flesh in three or four
gallons of water till it comes to a strong jelly, and that the
meat is good for nothing. Be sure to keep the pot close
covered, and not to do too fast; take a little out in a spoon
now and then, and when you find it is a good rich jelly,
strain it through a sieve into a clean earthen pan. When
it is cold, take off all the skin and fat from the top, then
provide a large deep stew-pan with water boiling over
a stove, then take some deep china-cups, or well-glazed
earthen-ware, and fill these cups with the jelly, which you
must take clear from the settling at the bottom, and set
them in the stew-pan of water. Take great care that none
of the water gets into the cups; if it does it will spoil it.
Keep the water boiling gently all the time till the jelly
becomes as thick as glue, take them out, and let them
stand to cool, and then turn the glue out into some new
coarse flannel, which draws out all the moisture, turn
them in six or eight hours on fresh flannel, and so do till
they are quite dry. Keep it in a dry warm place, and in a

little time it will be like a dry hard piece of glue, which you may carry in your pocket without getting any harm. The best way is to put it into little tin-boxes. When you use it, boil about a pint of water, and pour it on a piece of glue about as big as a small walnut, stirring it all the time till it is melted. Season with salt to your palate; and if you chuse any herbs or spice, boil them in the water first, and then pour the water over the glue.

Hannah Glasse, *The Art of Cookery Made Plain and Easy*, 1747

♣ Hannah Glasse's instant stock recipe is just one of many for homemade 'stock cubes' to be found in household manuals in the eighteenth century and the first half of the nineteenth. By the 1860s and 1870s companies like the Liebig Extract of Meat Company, whose factory opened in 1865, began to produce a factory-made meat extract. Liebig set up in the port of Fray Bentos in Uruguay, where they took advantage of meat from cattle being raised for their hide, at one-third the price of European meat. In the 1870s, John Lawson Johnston invented 'Johnston's Fluid Beef', later renamed Bovril. Unlike Liebig's meat extract, Bovril also contained flavourings and was manufactured in Argentina, which could also provide cheap cattle.

Hannah Glasse's poisonous purple pears

To STEW PEARS PURPLE. Pare four pears, cut them
into quarters, core them, put them into a stew-pan, with
a quarter of a pint of water, a quarter of a pound of sugar,
cover them with a pewter-plate, then cover the pan with
the lid, and do them over a slow fire. Look at them often,
for fear of melting the plate; when they are enough, and
the liquor looks of a fine purple, take them off, and lay
them in your dish with the liquor; when cold, serve
them up for a side-dish at a second course, or just as you
please.

Hannah Glasse, *The Art of Cookery Made Plain and Easy*, 1747

♣ A charming conceit not too far away from pears in red
wine, but, whatever you do, please don't try this at home,
unless you want to risk poisoning. Glasse's recipe unwittingly
used the chemical reaction between the acidic fruit and the
lead in the pewter to produce the purple colour change – a
change that would render the pears potentially poisonous.

To cook eggs in a butter whirlpool, make one giant egg using bladders and golden fairy butter to look like vermicelli

TO FRY EGGS AS ROUND AS BALLS. Having a deep frying-pan, and three pints of clarified butter, heat it as hot as for fritters, and stir it with a stick, till it runs round like a whirlpool; then break an egg into the middle, and turn it round with your stick, till it be as hard as a poached egg; the whirling round of the butter will make it as round as a ball; then take it up with a slice, and put it into a dish before the fire; they will keep hot half an hour, and yet be soft; so you may do as many as you please. You may poach them in boiling water in the same manner.

TO MAKE AN EGG AS BIG AS TWENTY. Part the yolks from the whites, strain them both separate through a sieve, tie the yolks up in a bladder in the form of a ball. Boil them hard, then put this ball into another bladder, and the whites round it; tie it up oval fashion, and boil it. These are used for grand sallads. This is very pretty for a ragoo [*from the French ragout, or stew*], boil five or six yolks together, and lay in the middle of the ragoo of eggs; and so you may make them of any size you please.

To Make Fairy Butter. Take the yolks of two hard eggs, and beat them in a marble mortar, with a large spoonful of orange-flower water, and two tea spoonfuls of fine sugar beat to powder; beat this all together till it is a fine paste, then mix it up with about as much fresh butter out of the churn, and force it through a fine strainer full of little holes into a plate. This is a pretty thing to set off a table at supper.

Hannah Glasse, *The Art of Cookery Made Plain and Easy*, 1747

♣ These three recipes, which all utilise eggs, show that the playful nature of medieval, Tudor and Stuart food was still alive in the Georgian period. These creations took skill and time to execute correctly and they perhaps reflect the nature of the audience that Hannah Glasse intended to reach. She had developed a writing style that adapted some of the more arcane language of earlier publications, which were often aimed at professional cooks, and she simplified instructions for the domestic cook. But some of the recipes for highly decorative foods are very complex and only a cook employed in a wealthier household would have had the spare time and the assistance to bring them to completion.

Artificial asses' milk
made with bruised snails

To Make artificial Asses-milk. Take two
ounces of pearl-barley, two large spoonfuls of hartshorn
[*ammonium carbonate, a forerunner of baking soda, made
from deer antlers*] shavings, one ounce of eringo [*sea
holly*] root, one ounce of China root [*edible root of the herb
Smilax china*], one ounce of preserved ginger, eighteen
snails bruised with the shells, to be boiled in three quarts
of water, till it comes to three pints, then boil a pint of
new milk, mix it with the rest, and put in two ounces
of balsam of Tolu [*a tree resin sometimes used to treat
coughs*]. Take half a pint in the morning, and half a pint at
night.

Hannah Glasse, The Art of Cookery Made Plain and Easy, 1747

♣ There are many recipes for artificial milks in old herbals,
household instruction books and cookbooks. Some milks
were in great demand for their medicinal properties, and
supply of the real thing could not keep up with demand.
Asses' milk was used to treat those weakened by consumption
as well as being given to the frail and the elderly.
Interestingly, modern analysis of mares' milk shows that its
proportions of fat, sugar and protein are very close to that

of human milk, whereas cows' milk is much higher in fat and protein but lower in sugar. The addition to the recipe of snails with their shells could reflect a basic understanding of the value of the calcium found in real animal milk.

A barrel of tripe
to take to the East Indies

To Preserve Tripe to go to the East-Indies.
Get a fine belly of tripe [*stomach lining*], quite fresh. Take
a four gallon cask well hooped, lay in your tripe, and have
your pickle ready made thus; take seven quarts of spring
water, and put as much salt into it as will make an egg
swim, that the little end of the egg may be about an inch
above the water (you must take care to have the fine clear
salt, for the common salt will spoil it); add a quart of the
best white vinegar, two sprigs of rosemary, an ounce of allspice, pour it on your tripe; let the cooper fasten the cask
down directly; when it comes to the Indies, it must not be
opened till it is just a-going to be dressed; for it wont keep
after the cask is opened. The way to dress it is, lay it in
water half and hour; then fry or boil it as we do here.

Hannah Glasse, *The Art of Cookery Made Plain and Easy*, 1747

❧ Recipes for the preservation of food continued to take up
a lot of space in cookery and household instruction books
in the eighteenth century. The books also reflected Britain's
influence overseas as she expanded her colonies and founded
an empire. It was a two-way phenomenon, with British food
and ideas going one way and new recipes and ingredients
coming back the other. Throughout the next two hundred
years India, in particular, was to export food ideas like
ketchup and chutney, which were quickly adopted and are
now considered as almost totally British (see next recipes).
But was there any necessity for the British Empire builders to
export barrels of tripe, of all things, to the East Indies? Tripe
would have been readily available wherever there were pigs,
cows and sheep, and surely anything would be better than
a barrel of tripe that had made a nine-month journey across
tropical seas.

A ketchup that will last you twenty years and an eighteenth-century Worcestershire sauce

To Make Catchup to Keep Twenty Years. Take a gallon of strong stale beer, one pound of anchovies washed from the pickle, a pound of shalots, peeled, half an ounce of mace, half an ounce of cloves, a quarter of an ounce of whole pepper, three or four large races [*dried roots*] of ginger, two quarts of the large mushroom-flaps rubbed to pieces. Cover all this close, and let it simmer till it is half wasted, then strain it through a flannel-bag; let it stand till it is quite cold, then boile it. You may carry it to the Indies. A spoonful of this to a pound of fresh butter melted, makes a fine fish-sauce or in the room [*in place*] of gravy-sauce. The stronger and staler the beer is, the better the catchup will be.

Hannah Glasse, *The Art of Cookery Made Plain and Easy*, 1747

To Make Mum Catchup. To a quart of old mum [*beer brewed from wheat malt and flavoured with herbs*] put four ounces of anchovies, of mace, and nutmegs sliced, one ounce of cloves, and black pepper half an ounce, boil it till it is reduced one third; when cold bottle it for use.

Elizabeth Raffald, *The Experienced English Housekeeper*, 1778

♣ The origin of the modern word 'ketchup' (catchup, ketsup and catsup) is much debated and may come from a Chinese or Malay word. More than 2000 years ago the Romans relished a sauce similar to ketchup, though perhaps closer to Thai fish sauce, called *liquamen*. However, modern ketchup probably originated somewhere in the Far East and was surely brought to this country through the expansion of trade, particularly by the East India Company, in the seventeenth century. Elizabeth Raffald also included a recipe for a spicier version of this ketchup that would keep for seven years, suitable for carrying to the East Indies.

Both recipes show that English cooks adapted imported recipes by utilising locally available ingredients, like beer, and that the resulting sauces or their recipes were, in turn, exported back to émigrés working in the expanding Empire. Although mushroom ketchup can still be found in supermarkets today, it has, along with all the other varieties, lost out to the all-powerful latecomer tomato ketchup, which began to be the most popular version from the late nineteenth century onwards.

How to tell if waders, gulls and
dotterels are fresh or stale

To Chuse the Shuffler, Godwitz, Marrel,
Knots, Gulls, Dotters, And Wheatears. These
birds, when new, are limber footed; when stale, dry
footed: when fat, they have a fat rump; when lean, a close
and hard one; when young their legs are smooth; when
old, rough.

Eliza Smith, *The Compleat Housewife:*
or Accomplished Gentlewoman's Companion, 1758

♣ Many of the eighteenth- and nineteenth-century
housewives' manuals were aimed at the emerging middle
classes, where women were expected to take on the running
of a household and the instruction of servants and cooks. In
an age before proper food inspection and quality testing the
housewife needed to know the signs and indications of what
was fresh and what was not. The manuals are full of tips
for correctly identifying cuts of meat, the freshness of fish,
the ripeness of fruit and vegetables, as well as spotting the
signs of adulteration. Before the later nineteenth century, the
adulteration of foods was commonplace, with, for example,
chalk added to bulk up watered-down milk, and alum or even
ground-up bones added to whiten bread made with old or
poor-quality flour.

Chopped brain fritters

To MAKE BRAIN-CAKES. Take a handful of bread-crumbs, a little shred lemon-peel, pepper, salt, nutmeg, sweet-marjorum, parsley shred fine, and the yolks of three eggs; take the brains and skin them, boil and chop them small, so mix them all together; take a little butter in your pan when you fry them, and drop them in as you do fritters, and if they run in your pan put in a handful more of bread-crumbs.

Elizabeth Moxon, *English Housewifery Exemplified*, 1764

♣ The title of this recipe belies its delicate sophistication and the understanding of cooking techniques. The combination of ingredients is subtle and the instructions simple and fairly precise, with none of the vagueness of some earlier cookbooks. The decline in the eating of offal can be mapped in direct relation to the increase in wealth of the British population, who, given the choice, will often opt for more expensive and simply prepared cuts of meat.

Hens, fish, eggs, bacon, islands
and playing cards in jelly

HENS AND CHICKENS IN JELLY. Make some flummery
[*thickened milk pudding*] with a deal of sweet almonds
in it, colour a little of it brown with chocolate, and put
it into a mould the shape of a hen; then colour some
more flummery with the yolk of a hard egg beat as fine as
possible, leave part of your flummery white, then fill the
mould of seven chickens, three with white flummery and
three with yellow, and one the colour of the hen; when
they are cold turn them into a deep dish; put under and
round them lemon peel, boiled tender and cut like straw,
then put a little clear calf's foot jelly under them, to keep
them in their places, and let it stand till it is stiff, then fill
up your dish with more jelly. They are a pretty decoration
for a grand table.

Elizabeth Raffald, *The Experienced English Housekeeper*, 1778

♣ Mrs Raffald had a penchant for creating these dramatic centrepieces with animal and plant shapes set in bowls of jelly. Here she creates a hen and her chicks from flummery, originally an oatmeal-based pudding but by this date a much more sophisticated blancmange made from almonds or cream, in a nest of shredded lemon rind, all submerged in a pool of clear jelly. She also created a fish pool with fish, eggs and bacon on a bed of spinach, a rocky island, Solomon's Temple, even playing cards – all made from flummery and often submerged in clear pools of jelly. She even created small fish from a clear blancmange, gilded them with gold leaf and floated them in a punch bowl filled with thin jelly or wine so that they looked as though they were swimming.

ELIZABETH RAFFALD.

Published as the Act directs by I. R. Baldwin July 31. 1782.

THE EXPERIENCED

Englifh Houfekeeper,

For the USE and EASE of

Ladies, Houfekeepers, Cooks, &c.

Written purely from PRACTICE,

AND DEDICATED TO THE

Hon. Lady ELIZABETH WARBURTON,

Whom the Authour lately ferved as Houfekeeper:

Confifting of near Nine Hundred Original Receipts, moft of which never appeared in Print.

PART I. Lemon Pickle, Browning for all Sorts of Made Difhes, Soups, Fifh, Plain Meat, Game, Made Difhes both hot and cold, Pies, Puddings, &c. PART II. All Kinds of Confectionary, particularly the Gold and Silver Web for covering of Sweetmeats, and a Deffert of Spun Sugar, with Directions to fet out a Table in the moft elegant Manner, and in the modern Tafte; Floating Iflands, Fifh-Ponds, Tranfparent Puddings, Trifles, Whips, &c. PART III. Pickling, Potting, and Collaring, Wines, Vinegars, Catch-ups, Diftilling, with two moft valuable Receipts, one for refining Malt Liquors, the other for curing Acid Wines, and a correct Lift of every Thing in Seafon for every Month in the Year.

THE NINTH EDITION.

WITH AN ENGRAVED HEAD OF THE AUTHOR;

Alfo two PLANS of a GRAND TABLE of Two Covers; and A curious new invented FIRE STOVE, wherein any common Fuel may be burnt, inftead of Charcoal.

By ELIZABETH RAFFALD.

LONDON:
PRINTED FOR R. BALDWIN No. 47, IN PATER-NOSTER-ROW,
MDCCLXXXIV.

Rabbits with jaw-bone horns,
a bunch of myrtle in their mouths
and a frothy liver sauce

RABBITS SURPRISED. Take young rabbits, skewer them, and put the same pudding into them as directed for roasted rabbits. When they be roasted, draw out the jaw-bones, and stick them in the eyes, to appear like horns. Then take off the meat clean from the bones; but the bones must be left whole. Chop the meat very fine, with a little shred parsley, some lemon-peel, an ounce of beef marrow, a spoonful of cream, and a little salt. Beat up the yolks of two eggs boiled hard, and a small piece of butter, in a marble mortar; then mix all together, and put it into a tossing pan. Having stewed it five minutes, lay it on the rabbit where you took the meat off, and put it close down with your hand, to make it appear like a whole rabbit. Then with a salamander [*see opposite*] brown it all over. Pour a good brown gravy, made as thick as cream, into the dish, and stick a bunch of myrtle in their mouths. Send them up to table, with their livers boiled and frothed.

John Farley, *The London Art of Cookery*, 1800

♣ In medieval times only rabbits under the age of one year were actually called by that name, otherwise they were conies. Rabbit was something of a luxury meat until early modern times, when they became more common and were kept, up until the eighteenth century, in warrens. This recipe deconstructs the rabbit, retaining the bones as a framework on which to reconstruct a rabbit pâté body enriched with bone-marrow, cream and lemon – to which was added the somewhat horrific detail of sticking the jawbones in the eyes in imitation of antlers. Given the delicate nature of the reconstituted rabbit, it was necessary to complete the final browning using a salamander. This tool was constructed of a solid disk of iron attached to a long handle; the disk was heated until red hot in the fire and then passed over the dish, browning the meat without actually touching it. With skill, the level of browning could be precisely controlled. Salamanders were commonly used for creating the caramelised sugar toppings on puddings like crème brûlée.

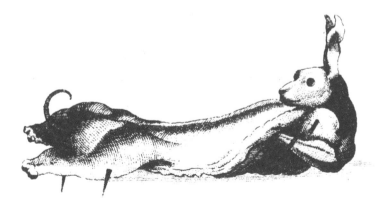

How to turn a live turtle into soup
and serve it in its shell

HOW TO COOK REAL TURTLE. Hang the turtle up
by the hind fins, and cut off the head overnight; in the
morning cut off the fore fins at the joints, and the callipee
all round; then take out the entrails, and be careful not to
break the gall; after which cut off the hind fins and all the
meat from the bones, callipee and calipash [*the gelatinous
substances in the upper and lower shells of the turtle, the
calipash being of a dull greenish and the calipee of a light
yellow colour*]; then chop the callipee and callipash into
pieces; scald them together, the fins being whole, but
take care not to let the scales set. When cleaned, chop

the fins into pieces four inches long; wash the pieces of
the callipee, callipash, and fins, and put them into a pot
with the bones and a sufficient quantity of water to cover;
then add a bunch of sweet herbs and whole onions, and
skim it when the liquor boils. When the fins are nearly
done take them out, together with the remainder of the
turtle, when done, picked free from bone. Then strain the
liquor and boil it down till reduced to one third part; after
which cut the meat into pieces four times larger than dice;
put it into a pot, add a mixture of herbs chopped fine,
such as knotted marjoram, savory, thyme, parsley, a very
little basil, some chopped onions, some beaten spices,
as allspice, a few cloves, a little mace, black pepper, salt,
some veal stock, and the liquor that was reduced. Boil the
meat till three parts done, pick it free from herbs, strain
the liquor through a tamis sieve, make a passing of flour
and three quarters of a pound of fresh butter, mixing it
well over a fire for some time, and then add to it madeira
wine (if a turtle of seventy pounds weight, three pints)
and the liquor of the meat. When it boils, skim it clean,
season to the palate with cayenne pepper, lemon juice, and
salt, and strain it to the pieces of fins and shell in one pot,
and the lean meat into another; and if the turtle produce
any real green fat, let it be boiled till done, then strained,
cut in pieces, and added to the fins and shell, and then

simmer each meat till tender. When it is to be served up, put a little fat at the bottom of the tureens, some lean in the centre, and more fat at the top, with egg and forcemeat balls, and a few entrails.

John Mollard, The Art of Cookery, 1808

❧ Turtle soup was one of the most fashionable dishes of the later Georgian and early Victorian period. It was in great demand at state and civic banquets, and was a particular speciality at the London Tavern, where live turtles were kept just for the purposes of making the soup. Because the animal had to be kept alive until the last minute, and due to its large size and the complexity of preparation, it was an expensive dish to create at home. It was one of the first foods to be prepared and sold in tins, along with its imitator, 'mock turtle soup', which was usually made with veal. The earliest recipe for real turtle soup appeared in the fourth edition of Hannah Glasse's *Art of Cookery* (1751) and the mock-turtle version came along just a few years later in the sixth edition of 1758.

A hairy heart for Valentine's Day

LOVE IN DISGUISE. After well cleaning, stuff a calf's heart, cover it an inch thick with good forcemeat [*stuffing*], then roll it in vermicelli, put it into a dish with a little water, and send it to the oven. When done, serve it with its own gravy in the dish. This forms a pretty side dish.

Mary Holland, *The Economical Cook and Frugal Housewife*, 1830

A Victorian savoury cheese ice cream

CHEESE (PARMESAN) ICE CREAM. Take six eggs,
half a pint of syrup and a pint of cream; put them into
a stewpan and boil them until it begins to thicken; then
rasp three ounces of parmesan cheese; mix the whole
well together and pass it through a sieve, then freeze it
according to custom.

Eliza Acton, *Modern Cookery for Private Families*, 1845

♣ Ice cream was highly fashionable in the late eighteenth and
early nineteenth centuries, when the confectionery trade in
London was dominated by a number of Italian confectioners,
including Domenico Negri and William Alexis Jarrin. Ices
were produced in many flavours, though this combination
of a sweet cream flavoured with three ounces of parmesan is
unusual and must have been an acquired taste.

SPECIMENS FROM
THE BOOK OF MOULDS,
Containing 68 pages of Illustrations, published by
MARSHALL'S SCHOOL OF COOKERY
And sent POST FREE on application.

BY ROYAL LETTERS PATENT.
MARSHALL'S PATENT FREEZER.

IS PRAISED BY ALL WHO KNOW IT

FOR

CHEAPNESS in first cost.
CLEANLINESS in working.
ECONOMY in use.
SIMPLICITY in construction.
RAPIDITY in Freezing.
No Packing necessary. No Spatula
necessary.
*Smooth and Delicious Ice produced in three
minutes.*

COMPLETE VIEW.

SIZES—No. 1, to freeze any quantity up to 1 quart, £1. 5s. ; No. 2, for 2 quarts, £1. 15s. ; No. 3, for 4 quarts,
£3 ; No. 4, for 6 quarts, £4. Larger sizes to order.

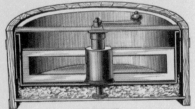

VERTICAL SECTION.
Shewing the fan inside, which remains still while the pan revolves and scrapes up the film of ice as it forms on
the bottom of the pan.
The ice and salt is also shewn *under* the pan ; there is no need to pack any round the sides.

PATENT ICE BREAKER.

No. 3, Price £3 each.
Will take a piece of ice about
5 inches by 6 inches by 8 inches,
breaking it into pieces about the
size of chestnuts.

No. 4, Price £1. 10s. each.
Will take a piece of ice about
4 inches by 4 inches by 6 inches,
and breaks it into very small
pieces.

Y Y

117

The swim bladder of a cod
served with egg sauce

To Boil Cod's Sounds [*the floatation bladder of the fish*]. Should they be highly salted, soak them for a night, and on the following day rub off entirely the discoloured skin; wash them well, lay them into plenty of cold milk and water, and boil them gently from thirty to forty minutes, or longer should they not be quite tender. Clear off the scum as it rises with great care, or it will sink and adhere to the sounds, of which the appearance will then be spoiled. Drain them well, dish them on a napkin, and send egg sauce and plain melted butter to table with them.

Eliza Acton, *Modern Cookery for Private Families*, 1845

❧ Virtually every part of the cod can be used in the kitchen and recipes can be found for cod cheeks, tongues, head and shoulders (see p. 130) and the roe. But it is hard to imagine that the swim-bladder could provide much nourishment unless it includes the muscles which work the bladder. However, Eliza Acton was a sensible and practical cookery writer and if she suggests serving them with an egg sauce then they must have been worth trying, even if they were meant for the more frugal and perhaps more easily pleased early Victorian housewife.

The flavour and texture of mature cheese created with eggs and spices

CHEESE ARTIFICIAL. Well pound some nutmeg, mace, and cinnamon, to which add a gallon of new milk, two quarts of cream, boil these in the milk, then put in eight eggs, six or eight spoonfuls of wine vinegar to turn the milk, let it boil till it comes to a curd, tie it up in a cheese cloth, and let it hang six or eight hours to drain, then open it, take out the spice, sweeten it with sugar and rose water, put it into a cullender, let it stand an hour more, then turn it out and serve it up in a dish with cream under it.

Frederick Bishop, *The Illustrated London Cookery Book*, 1852

♣ This really is something of a double bluff as the artificial cheese is in fact a real cheese, even if it is one whose flavour and texture are achieved by taking some shortcuts. It is, in effect, freshly made curd cheese with added spices, eggs and sugar. It was clearly meant to be served as a dessert and would have resembled an uncooked cheesecake.

A sweet 'cocktail' of sherry, port and chocolate

CHOCOLATE WINE. Take a pint of sherry or a pint and a half of port, four ounces and a half of chocolate, six ounces of fine sugar, and half an ounce of white starch or flour, mix, dissolve, and boil these altogether for ten or twelve minutes; but if your chocolate is made with sugar, take double the quantity of chocolate and half the quantity of sugar.

Frederick Bishop, *The Illustrated London Cookery Book*, 1852

♣ This is another recipe that has been rediscovered and reinvented by chef Heston Blumenthal, who acknowledges that versions of this recipe had been around since at least the late seventeenth century when cooks began to experiment with the newly introduced chocolate. Blumenthal's recipe has a very similar basis to that given here, but he finishes the drink by spinning the wine and chocolate mixture in a centrifuge, to separate the solids, before adding whey powder, instead of the starch of the original recipe, to produce a frothy head on the wine.

Arctic jelly

ICELAND MOSS JELLY. Wash four ounces of Iceland
moss in some warm water, strain off the water, and put
the moss on to boil in a quart of water, stirring it on the
fire until it boils; it must then be removed to the side,
covered over, and allowed to simmer gently for an hour;
then add four ounces of sugar, a gill of sherry, the juice
of two lemons, the peel of half a lemon, and a white of
egg whisked with half a gill of cold water; stir the jelly on
the fire until it boils, and pour it into a flannel jellybag;
when passed tolerably clear, it may be taken warm, in
which state it is most beneficial, or it may be eaten cold
like any other jelly. It is necessary to add, that washing
the moss deprives it of its tonic powers; and it is therefore
recommended to put up with the bitter taste for the sake
of its benefit. Iceland moss is very generally used on the
Continent in the treatment of consumption; it is most
active in the cure of severe coughs, and all phlegmatic
diseases of the chest.

Charles Francatelli, *A Plain Cookery Book
for the Working Classes*, 1852

♣ Iceland moss is actually a lichen, which in past times was used in soups, stews and porridge recipes. It grows on northern hills in England and throughout highland Scotland and most of the higher, colder parts of northern Europe and North America. It is still used in some folk medicines and, as Francatelli points out, was once considered useful for the treatment of consumption.

Mrs Beeton's nourishing soup for the deserving poor

USEFUL SOUP FOR BENEVOLENT PURPOSES.

Ingredients: An ox-cheek, any pieces of trimmings of beef, which may be bought very cheaply (say 4 lbs.), a few bones, any pot-liquor the larder may furnish, ½ peck of onions, 6 leeks, a large bunch of herbs, ½ lb. of celery (the outside pieces, or green tops, do very well); ½ lb. of carrots, ½ lb. of turnips, ½ lb. of coarse brown sugar, ½ a pint of beer, 4 lbs. of common rice, or pearl barley; ½ lb. of salt, 1 oz. of black pepper, a few raspings [breadcrumbs], 10 gallons of water.

Mode: Cut up the meat in small pieces, break the bones, put them in a copper, with the 10 gallons of water, and stew for ½ an hour. Cut up the vegetables, put them in with the sugar and beer, and boil for 4 hours. Two hours before the soup is wanted, add the rice and raspings, and keep stirring till it is well mixed in the soup, which simmer gently. If the liquor reduces too much, fill up with water.

Mrs Isabella Beeton, *Book of Household Management*, 1861

♣ Recipes for nourishing soups for the poor became a fashionable addition to the cookbook from the late eighteenth century onwards. Under the influence of the Christian Evangelical movement, ladies of leisure, like many of Jane Austen's heroines, were expected to make charitable visits to the poor, armed with soup and medicines made from recipes in the latest housewife's manual. The fashion continued into the nineteenth century, and in the winter of 1858 Mrs Isabella Beeton, as fitting a middle-class Victorian lady, made each week in her copper eight or nine gallons of this soup for distribution among about a dozen families of the village close to her home in Hatch End near Pinner in Middlesex. She had reason to believe, she said, 'that the soup was very much liked, and gave to the members of those families, a dish of warm, comforting food, in place of the cold meat and piece of bread which form, with too many cottagers, their usual meal, when, with a little more knowledge of the "cooking" art, they might have, for less expense, a warm dish, every day.'

Mrs Beeton's extremely economical soup for children

MILK SOUP (a Nice Dish for Children). 2 quarts of milk, 1 saltspoonful of salt, 1 teaspoonful of powdered cinnamon, 3 teaspoonfuls of pounded sugar, or more if liked, 4 thin slices of bread, the yolks of 6 eggs. Boil the milk with the salt, cinnamon, and sugar; lay the bread in a deep dish, pour over it a little of the milk, and keep it hot over a stove, without burning. Beat up the yolks of the eggs, add them to the milk, and stir it over the fire till it thickens. Do not let it curdle. Pour it upon the bread, and serve. Average cost, 8*d*. per quart. Seasonable all the year. Sufficient for 10 children.

Mrs Isabella Beeton, *Book of Household Management*, 1861

♣ This soup was intended for use in the nursery, rather than for distribution around the houses of the poor, and would have been served either as a breakfast or tea-time dish. The great Victorian chef and caterer Alexis Soyer suggested the following menu for those who had children in their care: 'Bread and milk at eight; dinner at one: roast mutton and apple pudding; roast beef and currant pudding; boiled mutton with turnips, and rice or vermicelli pudding; occasionally a little salt beef with suet dumplings, plain or with currants in them or pease pudding … and to these we should add bread and butter and milk and water for tea, and a fair meal of bread and cheese or butter for supper.'

Mrs Beeton's stock cubes

PORTABLE SOUP. 2 knuckles of veal, 3 shins of beef, 1 large faggot [*bundle*] of herbs, 2 bay-leaves, 2 heads of celery, 3 onions, 3 carrots, 2 blades of mace, 6 cloves, a teaspoonful of salt, sufficient water to cover all the ingredients. Take the marrow from the bones; put all the ingredients in a stock-pot, and simmer slowly for 12 hours, or more, if the meat be not done to rags; strain it off, and put it in a very cool place; take off all the fat, reduce the liquor in a shallow pan, by setting it over a sharp fire, but be particular that it does not burn; boil it fast and uncovered for 8 hours, and keep it stirred. Put it into a deep dish, and set it by for a day. Have ready a stewpan of boiling water, place the dish in it, and keep it boiling; stir occasionally, and when the soup is thick and ropy, it is done. Form it into little cakes by pouring a small quantity on to the bottom of cups or basins; when cold, turn them out on a flannel to dry. Keep them from the air in tin canisters. Average cost of this quantity, 16*s*.

Mrs Isabella Beeton, *Book of Household Management*, 1861

♣ As this recipe demonstrates, little had changed in the domestic production of meat extract since Hannah Glasse's recipe of a hundred years earlier (see p. 95). But by the early twentieth century, the company Liebig had changed their commercial liquid meat extract into a dry stock cube, which they now marketed under the brand name OXO. In 1908 OXO sponsored the London Olympic Games (despite claims by Coca-Cola to being the first commercial sponsor of the Olympics) and supplied athletes with OXO drinks to fortify them.

Making a meal of a cod's head and shoulders (including carving instructions)

COD'S HEAD AND SHOULDERS. Sufficient water to cover the fish; 5 oz. of salt to each gallon of water. Cleanse the fish thoroughly, and rub a little salt over the thick part and inside of the fish, 1 or 2 hours before dressing it, as this very much improves the flavour. Lay it in the fish-kettle, with sufficient cold water to cover it. Be very particular not to pour the water on the fish, as it is liable to break it, and only keep it just simmering. If the water should boil away, add a little by pouring it in at the side of the kettle, and not on the fish. Add salt in the above proportion, and bring it gradually to a boil. Skim very carefully, draw it to the side of the fire, and let it gently simmer till done. Take it out and drain it; serve on a hot napkin, and garnish with cut lemon, horseradish, the roe and liver. Average cost, from 3s. to 6s. Sufficient for 6 or 8 persons. Seasonable from November to March.   NOTE. Oyster sauce and plain melted butter should be served with this.

CARVING A COD'S HEAD AND SHOULDERS. First run the knife along the centre of the side of the fish, namely, from *d* to *b*, down to the bone; then carve it in unbroken slices downwards from *d* to *e*, or upwards from *d* to *c*, as

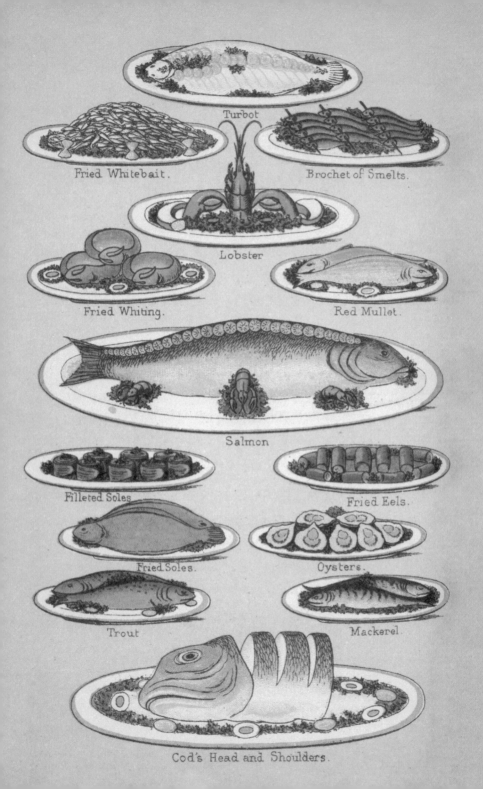

Turbot

Fried Whitebait.

Brochet of Smelts.

Lobster

Fried Whiting.

Red Mullet.

Salmon

Filleted Soles

Fried Eels.

Fried Soles.

Oysters.

Trout

Mackerel.

Cod's Head and Shoulders.

shown in the engraving. The carver should ask the guests if they would like a portion of the roe and liver.

NOTE. Of this fish, the parts about the backbone and shoulders are the firmest, and most esteemed by connoisseurs. The sound, which lines the fish beneath the backbone, is considered a delicacy, as are also the gelatinous parts about the head and neck.

Mrs Isabella Beeton, *Book of Household Management*, 1861

♣ Samuel Pepys notes in his diary that he shared and enjoyed a cod's head with Sir William Batton, Surveyor of the Kings Navy, on 23 January 1663. *Routledge's Manual of Etiquette* in the nineteenth century opined that, next to turbot, a cod's head and shoulders is the handsomest dish of fish brought to the table. This dish has thus been highly regarded for hundreds of years and it would be remarkable that it had fallen out of favour were it not for one very significant factor. With the overfishing of cod in the North Atlantic and the collapse of fish stocks on the east coast of Canada, it is very rare for a cod's head of sufficient size to reach the fishmonger's slab that could be utilised in this dish. Most modern cods' heads and shoulders would provide little more than a mouthful for one, let alone a dinner for two. Cod cheeks have found their way back onto the modern British menu, as a high-class tasty morsel, but it may be a long time before the head and shoulders make a return as a major dish for sharing.

A cheap pudding
for soldiers and sailors on half-pay

HALF-PAY PUDDING. ¼ lb. of suet, ¼ lb. of currants, ¼ lb. of raisins, ¼ lb. of flour, ¼ lb. of bread crumbs, 2 tablespoonfuls of treacle, ½ pint of milk. Chop the suet finely; mix with it the currants, which should be nicely washed and dried, the raisins, which should be stoned, the flour, bread crumbs, and treacle; moisten with the milk, beat up the ingredients until all are thoroughly mixed, put them into a buttered basin, and boil the pudding for 3-½ hours. Average cost, 8*d*. Sufficient for 5 or 6 persons. Seasonable at any time.

Mrs Isabella Beeton, *Book of Household Management*, 1861

♣ Half-pay refers to the pay or allowance an officer, particularly a Royal Navy officer, received when in retirement or not on active service. Jane Austen's Captain Harville in her novel *Persuasion* is a classic example of such an officer, living without a command on half-pay in Lyme Regis with his wife and children, trying to make do and mend in a rented house whilst he awaits a call to return to sea.

133

To make a pint of gruel for invalids

TO MAKE GRUEL. 1 tablespoonful of Robinson's patent
groats [*oats*], 2 tablespoonfuls of cold water, 1 pint of
boiling water. Mix the prepared groats smoothly with the
cold water in a basin; pour over them the boiling water,
stirring it all the time. Put it into a very clean saucepan;
boil the gruel for 10 minutes, keeping it well stirred;
sweeten to taste, and serve. It may be flavoured with a
small piece of lemon-peel, by boiling it in the gruel, or a
little grated nutmeg may be put in; but in these matters
the taste of the patient should be consulted. Pour the
gruel in a tumbler and serve. When wine is allowed to
the invalid, 2 tablespoonfuls of sherry or port make this
preparation very nice. In cases of colds, the same quantity
of spirits is sometimes added instead of wine. Sufficient to
make a pint of gruel.

Mrs Isabella Beeton, *Book of Household Management*, 1861

♣ Mr Woodhouse, the invalid father of Jane Austen's Emma, spent much of his time eating gruel. If he was lucky, his doctor would allow the addition of a tablespoon of wine. Gruel is really a variation on porridge, though sometimes the actual oats were strained out and the resulting liquid allowed to cool and turn to jelly. Apart from the addition of wine or sugar and depending on the condition of the invalid, pounded pork or juices extracted from beef might be added. By the second quarter of the nineteenth century gruel had become the staple food of the workhouse, and it is gruel, no doubt without any additions, that Oliver Twist asks for more of in Dickens's novel.

How to avoid making an
exceedingly disagreeable beverage

TO MAKE TOAST-AND-WATER. A slice of bread, 1 quart
of boiling water. Cut a slice from a stale loaf (a piece of
hard crust is better than anything else for the purpose),
toast it off a nice brown on every side, but do not allow
it to burn or blacken. Put it into a jug, pour the boiling
water over it, cover it closely, and let it remain until cold.
When strained, it will be ready for use. Toast-and-water
should always be made a short time before it is required,
to enable it to get cold: if drunk in a tepid or lukewarm
state, it is an exceedingly disagreeable beverage. If, as is
sometimes the case, this drink is wanted in a hurry, put
the toasted bread into a jug, and only just cover it with the
boiling water; when this is cool, cold water may be added
in the proportion required, the toast-and-water strained;
it will then be ready for use, and is more expeditiously
prepared than by the above method.

Mrs Isabella Beeton, *Book of Household Management*, 1861

♣ Toast and water or bread and water were seen as suitable foods for the invalid, but in the 'Hungry Forties' which followed a series of disastrous harvests in the middle of the nineteenth century, some of the poor survived on brewis, known in Lancashire as 'Bolton brewis'. It was made by pouring boiling water over a crust of bread; the water was then poured off and the bread sprinkled with salt and pepper. In slightly better times, another kind of brewis was made with the water in which pork had been boiled. It was poured over oatcakes, which were then mashed, seasoned with salt and pepper and served by themselves or with black pudding.

How to cook birds' nests as white as snow (*pick out any small feathers first*)

SWALLOWS' NEST SOUP. This soup is in reality much simpler of preparation than its ambitious name would lead one to imagine. I give it here on account of its originality; and I think I may venture to say, that its principal merit, irrespective of its outlandish element, is due to the *consommé* employed in its preparation. For soup for 12 persons, steep, say, 9 swallows' nests in water, for twenty-four hours; wash, and pick them very carefully; the nests will then be in shreds, very similar to *nouilles* [*noodles*]; pick out any small feathers which may still adhere to the nests, and wash them again several times, until they are as white as snow; put them in a stewpan, with 1 quart of General Stock, and simmer for two hours very gently; drain, and put the nests in a soup tureen, and pour over 2 quarts of boiling *consommé*, prepared as directed.

Jules Gouffé, *The Royal Cookery Book*, 1869

♣ Bird's-nest soup is made from the nest of a number of species of swiftlet found in Southeast Asia. The cup-shaped nests are composed of interwoven strands of the swift's saliva, though some have claimed that it is made of regurgitated seaweed and therefore contains agar-agar. The nests are dried and exported all over the world, as they must have been even in Jules Gouffé's day. Birds' nests are one of the world's most expensive ingredients and so in modern times only a tiny amount is used in a recipe. Gouffé's nine nests among twelve people would now seem extravagant.

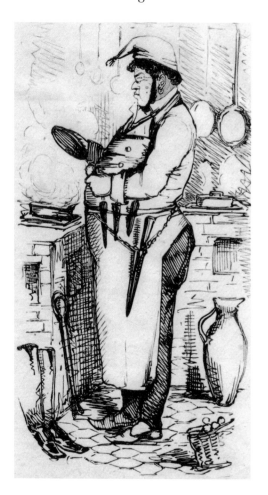

Tendons with all the meat removed
served in gravy with peas

TENDONS OF VEAL WITH GREEN PEAS. Cut the
tendons, or gristle, from 2 breasts of veal; blanch and cut
them into oval-shaped pieces 2 inches long; put them in
a glazing stewpan, with sufficient *consommé* and *mirepoix*
[*finely chopped vegetables*] to cover them entirely; simmer
till the tendons are done; when tried with a trussing
needle, it should enter freely; drain and press the tendons
between two dishes; strain the liquor in which they
have been cooked, free it of fat, and reduce it; when the
tendons are cold, trim off any remaining meat which
might be on them; warm them in the reduced gravy, and
dish them in a circle round a *croustade* [*pastry case*]; fill
the latter with green peas; pour some of the gravy over the
tendons; and serve the remainder in a boat.

Jules Gouffé, *The Royal Cookery Book*, 1869

♣ Tendons of veal may seem at first sight an unusually lowly recipe to appear in Gouffé's collection of high-class dishes. But similar recipes had long been a speciality of the Piedmont region of Italy and were so prized that the final dishes were enhanced with a whole truffle and decorated with cockscombs and slices of tongue cut into decorative shapes. The long, slow cooking and subsequent pressing of the tendons is very similar to the preparation of breast of lamb in England and France.

141

Kangaroo soup and curry,
roast wallaby and parakeet pie

Soup from Kangaroo Tails. Ingredients: 1 tail,
2 lbs. of beef, 3 carrots, 3 onions, a bunch of herbs,
pepper and salt, butter, water. Cut the tail into joints and
fry brown in butter; slice the vegetables and fry them also.
Put tail and vegetables into a stewpan with the meat cut
in slices and boil all for four hours in 3 quarts of water.
Take out the pieces of tail, strain the stock, thicken it with
flour, put back the pieces of tail and boil up for another
10 minutes before serving. Sufficient for eight persons.

Curried Kangaroo Tails. Ingredients: 1 tail, 2 oz.
of butter, 1 tablespoonful of flour, 1 tablespoonful of
curry-powder, 2 onions, sliced, 1 sour apple cut into dice,
1 dessert-spoonful of lemon juice, ¾ of a pint of stock,
salt. Method: Wash, blanch and dry the tail thoroughly,
and divide it at the joints. Fry the tail lightly in hot butter,
take it up, put in the sliced onions, and fry them for a
few minutes without browning. Sprinkle in the flour and
curry-powder, and cook gently for at least 20 minutes,
stirring frequently. Add the stock, bring to the boil,
stirring meanwhile, and replace the tail in the stewpan.
Cover closely, and cook gently until tender, then add the

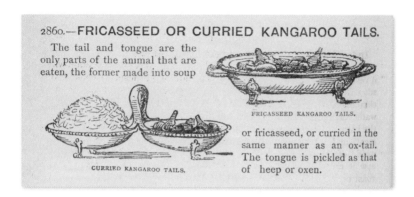

2860.—FRICASSEED OR CURRIED KANGAROO TAILS.
The tail and tongue are the only parts of the animal that are eaten, the former made into soup

FRICASSEED KANGAROO TAILS.

CURRIED KANGAROO TAILS.

or fricasseed, or curried in the same manner as an ox-tail. The tongue is pickled as that of heep or oxen.

lemon-juice and more seasoning if necessary. Arrange the pieces of tail on a hot dish, strain the sauce over, and serve with boiled rice. Time: from 2 to 3 hours.

ROAST WALLABY. Ingredients: wallaby, forcemeat [*stuffing*], milk, butter. Cut off the hind legs at the first joints and after skinning and paunching, let it lie in water for a little to draw out the blood. Make a good veal forcemeat and after well washing the inside of the wallaby, stuff it and sew it up. Truss as a hare and roast before a bright clear fire from 1½ to 1¾ hours, according to size. It must be kept some distance from the fire when first put down, or the outside will be too dry before the inside is done. Baste well, first with milk and then with butter and when nearly done dredge with flour and baste again with butter until nicely frothed.

PARROT PIE. Ingredients: 1 dozen paraqueets (small parrots), a few slices of cooked beef, 4 rashers of bacon, 3 hard-boiled eggs, minced parsley and lemon-peel, pepper and salt, stock, puff-paste. Line a pie-dish with the beef cut into slices, over them place 6 of the paraqueets, dredge with flour, fill up the spaces with egg cut in slices and scatter over the seasoning. Next put the bacon, cut in small strips, then 6 paraqueets and fill up with the beef, seasoning as well. Pour in stock or water to nearly fill the dish, cover with puff-pastry and bake for 1 hour.

Mrs Isabella Beeton, *Book of Household Management*, 1889

♣ Kangaroo was the staple meat of Aboriginal Australians and was quickly adopted by British settlers in the early colonial period. Because it was native to Australia kangaroo meat could be bought at half the price of beef in the markets of Sydney at the end of the eighteenth century. Early Australian cookbooks had many recipes for the meat and it found its way into later additions of Mrs Beeton. Beeton's reputation for including almost all forms of edible meat and vegetables in fact was only established after her early death, when the copyright of the book was bought by Ward Locke and vastly expanded in scope throughout the late nineteenth and early twentieth centuries. Kangaroo and wallaby meat fell out of favour in Australia in the twentieth century but has been revived as an environmentally sustainable meat in more recent years.

Parrot has been eaten by indigenous peoples across those parts of the world where it naturally occurs and, like kangaroo, was a feature of early colonial Australian cuisine. However, as reported by the food writer Alan Davidson, parrot and cockatoo recipes attracted little praise and were often the subject of jokes – 'cook a cockatoo with an old boot in plenty of boiling water until the boot is tender, then throw away the bird and eat the boot'.

On the naming of recipes

HORSE ARTILLERY PUDDING. ¾ lb sultanas, ½ lb suet chopped fine, ¼ citron chopped fine, a little nutmeg grated, 2 oz sugar, ½ teaspoon salt, 1 teaspoon flour, 3 eggs well beaten, 1 glass brandy. Butter well the mould and boil for 7 hours, not less. The pudding can always be boiled the day before, then heat up next day for use.

GUN TROOP SAUCE FOR PUDDINGS. One glass brandy, ¼ lb butter, ¼ lb sugar, yolk of an egg. All well beaten up together.

BUNNY HUGS. Make some pancakes, flavoured with salt. When cooked roll into each some minced mutton or beef, and send to table very hot. Serve thick gravy either round them or separately.

Rare Recipes, 'Collected by Deolee', 1912

♣ Many recipes have been given fanciful names to make them sound more attractive, to disguise their ingredients or to repackage an old, stolen recipe under a new title. In these recipes from 1912 there appears to be no connection between the Royal Artillery and the pudding or the sauce, which was presumably heated, and it is impossible to see why minced mutton wrapped in pancakes was christened 'Bunny Hugs'.

146

An economical savoury trifle

BEEF TRIFLE. 1 lb cold meat, chopped finely;
1 tablespoon horseradish, grated; 3 oz breadcrumbs;
½ onion, chopped; 2 oz margarine; 1 egg; pepper and salt
to taste. Mix well together. Place in small cups, greased.
Bake in moderate oven 20 minutes. Turn out on a hot dish
with gravy round.

Florence Petty, *The 'Pudding Lady's' Recipe Book*, 1917

The working-class tea and jazz-age cocktails

THE TEA OF THE ENGLISH WORKING CLASS is the most eccentric of meals, and one of the greatest injuries a gourmet could possibly conceive … for with the tea they partake of various kinds of salted meat and dried fish, such as 'corned-beef', kippers, bloaters, red herrings, winkles, shrimps, pickles, watercresses, cucumber, lettuce, jam or marmalade, bread and butter, and cake. This incongruous kind of food may, no doubt, be quite nice and tasty for this class of people, but it must shock anyone endowed with refined epicurean instinct.

J. Rey, *The Whole Art of Dining*, 1921

♣ The snobbery and social distinctions in this instructional caterer's manual – written just three years after the end of the Great War, in which millions of the European 'working classes' had been slaughtered, and following Prime Minister Lloyd George's promise to create a 'home fit for heroes to live in' – are astounding. The book's aim is to describe to the aspirational host and hostess the intricate details of the dining habits and traditions of the decadent classes. Apart from patronising the working classes, the book includes some very fashionable 'jazz age' drinks, including the following daringly named cocktails.

BOSOM CARESSER. Beat up a new-laid egg into a bowl, add a quarter of a pint of fresh milk, two spoonfuls of raspberry syrup, two liqueur-glasses of liqueur brandy, a glass of Curaçao, and three or four lumps of ice. Stir well and strain into a small tumbler.

LOVE'S REVIVER. Put into a sherry-glass a liqueur-glass of liqueur brandy, the yolk of a new-laid egg, two dashes of Kirsch, two dashes of maraschino and serve. (This should be drunk at a gulp.)

J. Rey, *The Whole Art of Dining*, 1921

Hedgehog cooked in a ball of clay

WAYS OF COOKING A HEDGEHOG. After killing the hedgehog, clean its inside. Then roll it thickly in some moist clay and put it in a moderate oven (Romany or kitchen oven) and bake till the clay is quite dry and hard. Break the clay by cracking it with a stick or hammer and the prickles and the top skin, which will adhere to the clay, will come off with it. Lastly, skin the legs. Having prepared the hedgehog as above, it can be cooked in different ways: either roasted or fried as a chicken, stewed as a rabbit, or made into pâté as for hare pâté.

Vicomte de Mauduit, *They Can't Ration These*, 1940

♣ The foraging for and cooking of wild foods are now highly fashionable, with some restaurants attempting to supply most of their ingredients from nature. During the Second World War it became a necessity for some to supplement their meagre rations with wild protein. This way of cooking hedgehogs, sometimes described as 'gypsy fashion', had been recorded long before the 1940s and had even found its way into Boy Scouts' survival manuals.

Several ways to cook squirrel, including a squirrel-tail soup

THE SQUIRREL. This is another delicacy, the flesh of a squirrel being more tasty and tender than that of a chicken.

GRILLED SQUIRREL. Skin and clean the squirrel, then open it out as you would a chicken for grilling, and grill the squirrel in the same way.

SQUIRREL-TAIL SOUP. The tail, which is put aside after skinning, can be used with haricot beans, onions, and herbs to make a delicious soup.

ROAST SQUIRREL. Squirrel is also most tasty roasted, and this is done in the same way as for roast chicken.

Vicomte de Mauduit, *They Can't Ration These*, 1940

151

How to avoid a bitter rook stew

STEWED ROOKS. Clean, draw [*eviscerate*], and skin the rooks. Make an incision half an inch thick on each side of the spine and remove this piece which is the bitter part of the rook. Put the birds in a casserole with equal parts of water and milk sufficient to cover the rooks, add salt, pepper, 1 sliced onion, 2 sliced turnips, 2 sliced carrots, some chopped mint or preferably chopped fennel, and stew with the lid on the pan until tender.

Vicomte de Mauduit, *They Can't Ration These*, 1940

♣ Along with instructions for cooking wild plants, fruits and vegetables, the author of *They Can't Ration These* included recipes for dealing with wild birds which take us right back to the recipes of medieval England. Under pressure, humans will get protein wherever they can, and there is no place for squeamishness in periods of severe food shortage, whether you are a medieval serf or a 1940s' family struggling to cope with rationing.

Vine-leaf wrapped sparrows
or starlings on toast

ROAST SPARROWS. Sparrows when roasted in this way are far from despicable. Pluck the birds and cut off the head and neck and feet. Draw [*eviscerate*] the birds from the neck end, then truss them as you would pigeons, cover breasts with slices of bacon, then (if available) wrap the bird in vine leaves and tie round with string. Roast for 15 minutes, basting frequently. During this time chop finely the birds' livers, fry them in a little of the birds' gravy, season to taste, spread thickly over pieces of fried toast, place one bird on each piece of toast and pour the gravy over all.

ROAST STARLINGS. After skinning the birds, clean them and roast them as you would sparrows.

Vicomte de Mauduit, They Can't Ration These, 1940

Freshly roasted asparagus coffee

COFFEE SUBSTITUTE. Gather the berries of the grown asparagus plant, dry them, and as and when required roast them in a coffee-roaster or in a hot oven. Grind them finely in a coffee-mill or pound them in a mortar and make coffee in the usual way. This nectar has a caramel flavour and is very agreeable to the taste. Roasted and ground chicory roots can be also added in the proportion of 1 teaspoonful for every 3 tablespoonfuls.

Vicomte de Mauduit, *They Can't Ration These*, 1940

♣ During the Napoleonic wars, when a shortage of the imported coffee bean arose, Napoleon offered a big prize for a substitute, and this was the winning recipe. The Vicomte de Mauduit would have been well informed about Napoleon's ideas as his great-grandfather, General de Mauduit, had accompanied the Emperor on his exile to St Helena. A similar food shortage had led Napoleon to encourage scientists in the search for an alternative to cane sugar, which was eventually found in sugar beet.

Eating with Pleasure

WAR-TIME COOKERY WITHOUT TEARS

By E. P. WHITE

1/-

A kitchen goes to war

AGATHA CHRISTIE'S MYSTERY POTATOES. 6 good-
sized potatoes, a little margarine, 4 tablespoonsful cream,
10 anchovies. Bake the potatoes in a moderate oven. Then
cut them in half, remove the insides and mash them with
the margarine and cream. Chop up the anchovies and mix
them in. Add pepper and salt to taste. Return mixture to
the empty skins, dap on top with margarine and brown in
a hot oven.

CHEESE AND CHUTNEY BISCUITS. Jack Warner
says: 'This may not be a "rill mill", but it is a quick,
satisfying snack.' Ingredients: 1 dozen water biscuits, 2 oz.
margarine or butter, 2 tablespoonsful chutney, about ¼ lb
cheese. Method: Spread the biscuits with margarine or
butter. Cover with cheese in slices and chutney.

SIR KENNETH CLARK'S HAM ROLL SALAD. 4 slices of
boneless cooked ham (cut thinly), 1 jar pâté de foie paste,
French mustard, 1 lettuce, 1 bunch watercress. Spread the
pâté on the cooked ham and then a little French mustard.
Roll up like a Swiss roll. Dish on a bed of lettuce and
garnish with sprigs of watercress.

*A Kitchen Goes to War: Famous People Contribute 150
Recipes to a Ration-time Cookery Book, 1940*

— AN EMERGENCY MEAL —

♣ In the government publication *A Kitchen Goes to War* (1940), 'celebrities' were asked to supply a favourite economical and practical recipe to help the war effort and demonstrate that 'we are all in this together'. Many of the recipes came from the wives of MPs and members of the government, but there were others that were a little more intriguing, or at least the byline promised more than it delivered. Sadly, the only mystery in Agatha Christie's potato dish is the title itself, and music-hall and radio star Jack Warner's 'cheese and crackers' must be one of the most basic 'recipes' ever published. In contrast, Sir Kenneth Clark, at the time director of the National Gallery, laughably suggests pâté de foie paste as an ingredient, leaving himself open to a cry of, 'Oi, mate, don't yer know there's a war on?'

Potato Pete's
recipe book

Potato Pete and Doctor Carrot

JACK-IN-THE-BOX. 6 medium well-scrubbed potatoes,
12 sprats, cooked cabbage. Make a hole lengthwise through
the centre of each potato, using an apple corer. Allowing
2 sprats for each potato, make one head emerge from one
side and the tail of the second fish appear from the other
end of the tunnel. Bake in the usual manner and serve on
a bed of cabbage dressed with a little vinegar, a grating of
nutmeg and a good shake of pepper.

Ministry of Food, *Potato Pete's Recipe Book*, *c.*1941

♣ The wartime government invented Potato Pete to encourage
the nation to eat as much of the 'off-ration' home-grown
vegetable as they could. Under his benign instruction, every
meal of the day could incorporate potatoes; in bread, scones,
savoury dishes and sweets. Many of the recipes were given
friendly names to hide their true nature, thus Jack-in-the-box
turns out to be sprats sticking out of holes in potatoes, served
on a bed of vinegar-sauced cabbage. No butter, no cheese, no
meat, just lovely, wholesome, dry potato with the accusing
eye of a fish peering from inside, daring you to complain.
Alongside Pete, the Ministry of Food also devised Doctor
Carrot and the myth that carrots helped you see in the dark
– allegedly to hide from the Germans how the British were
actually seeing in the dark using RADAR.

The hidden delights of cold porridge

LEMON CURD SANDWICHES. Sweet sandwiches made with bread do not seem quite the same as our old friend Sponge Sandwich, but they are very good. Make your sandwiches of national wheatmeal bread and spread them with one or other of these mixtures.

1. Make some porridge with fine oatmeal, and use this to thicken custard flavoured with lemon essence.

2. Make a very thick custard, and meanwhile toast some coarse oatmeal in the oven. When it is done, let it get cold and then mix it with the lemon-flavoured custard in whatever proportion you like. You will find it gives the 'spread' a very pleasantly 'nutty' flavour.

More Kitchen Front Recipes, 1942

♣ During the Second World War the British government promoted a system of food substitute recipes, calculated to provide the same or better nutritional value as popular dishes prepared in peacetime. Thus roast beef and Yorkshire pudding could be replaced with savoury vegetable roll, fish and chips by baked stuffed potatoes, and Victoria sponge cake with 'mock lemon curd' sandwiches. The true horror of some of these recipes can be demonstrated by that for the lemon curd, given in two delightful versions.

Further uses for cold porridge

SURPRISE CREAM WITH OAT CRISPS. Ingredients
– Cream: 2 teacups thick cold porridge, ½ tin evaporated
milk, ¼ oz. gelatine, 2 tablespoons castor sugar, vanilla
essence, colouring if liked, 2 oz. sultanas. Crisps: 1 oz.
flour, 1 oz. oatmeal, ¼ oz. lard, 1 teaspoon castor sugar,
pinch of cream of tartar, ¾ level teaspoon baking powder,
pinch salt, 1 tablespoon milk. Method: Whip [evaporated]
milk till thick, gradually whip in the cold porridge.
Dissolve gelatine in a little hot water, add to mixture
with castor sugar, vanilla essence and colouring. Whip
well and pour into glass dish. When set, decorate with
raisins. Serve with sweetened oat crisps. Crisps: Mix dry
ingredients and mix with milk, to a stiff consistency. Turn
out and stamp with an apple corer. Cut into lengths and
place on a greased tin. Bake in a moderately hot oven till
crisp and lightly browned.

Dainty Dishes for the Queen: Recipes of Oatmeal and Potato
Dishes used by Girls in the Scottish Primary Products
Contest, Scottish Education Department, 1944

⚓ In an effort to encourage the consumption of home-grown foods during the Second World War, the Scottish Education Department ran a competition to find the best recipe using oatmeal or potatoes. Margaret More, a schoolgirl from Kippen Public School and 20,000 competitors, became the Stirling County Champion with this winning recipe. But it comes as little surprise to learn that the 'surprise' ingredient in her not-so-dainty dish is two cups of thick cold porridge. More made it to the finals and got to meet King George and Queen Elizabeth in Glasgow. If this was a winning entry, what can the recipes have been like that didn't make it past the first round?

Picture sources

163

ACKNOWLEDGEMENTS The author would like to thank Lara Speicher, Sally Nicholls and Jenny Lawson for their assistance in this project.